MW00534474

Melody, Lyrics and Simplified Chords

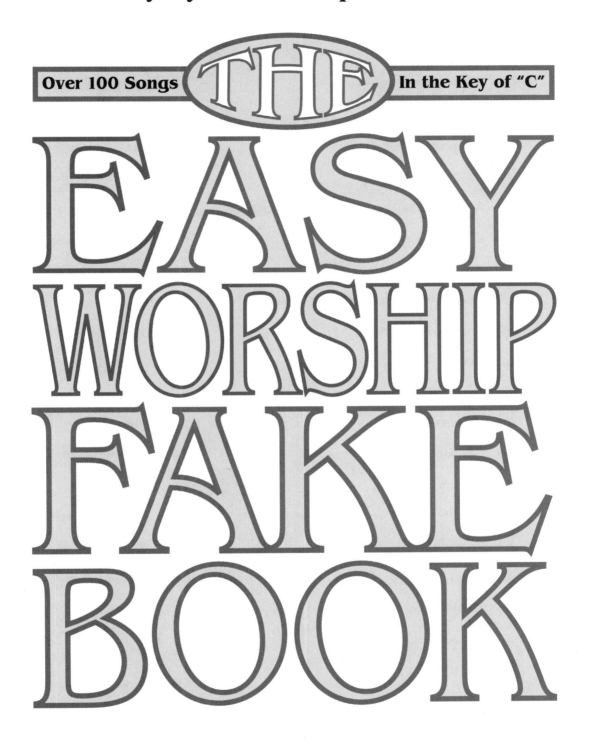

Over 100 Songs **THE** In the Key of "C"

EASY
WORSHIP
FAKE
BOOK

ISBN 978-1-61780-384-0

HAL•LEONARD®
CORPORATION
7777 W. BLUEMOUND RD. P.O. BOX 13819 MILWAUKEE, WI 53213

Visit Hal Leonard Online at
www.halleonard.com

MORE OF THE EASY WORSHIP FAKE BOOK

CONTENTS

INTRODUCTION

What Is a Fake Book?

A fake book has one-line music notation consisting of melody, lyrics and chord symbols.

This lead sheet format is a "musical shorthand" which is an invaluable resource for all musicians—hobbyists to professionals.

Here's how *The Easy Worship Fake Book* differs from most standard fake books:

- All songs are in the key of C.

- Many of the melodies have been simplified.

- Only five basic chord types are used—major, minor, seventh, diminished and augmented.

- The music notation is larger for ease of reading.

In the event that you haven't used chord symbols to create accompaniment, or your experience is limited, a chord speller chart is included at the back of the book to help you get started.

Have fun!

ALL THE EARTH WILL SING YOUR PRAISES

Words and Music by
PAUL BALOCHE

ALL WHO ARE THIRSTY

Words and Music by BRENTON BROWN
and GLENN ROBERTSON

All who are thirst-y, all who are ____ weak,

come to the foun-tain, dip your heart in the stream of

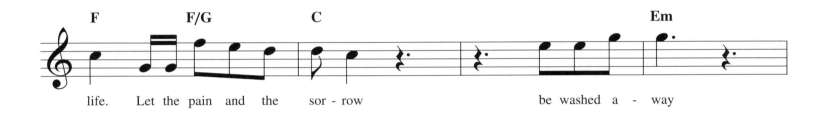

life. Let the pain and the sor-row be washed a - way

in the waves of His mer-cy, as deep cries out to

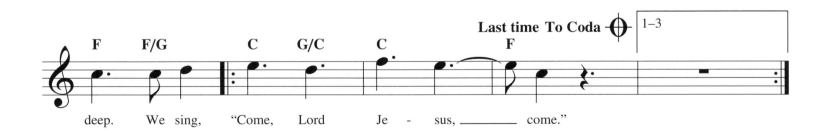

deep. We sing, "Come, Lord Je - sus, ____ come."

All who are

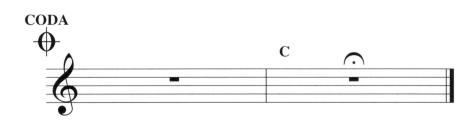

AMAZED

Words and Music by
JARED ANDERSON

ANCIENT WORDS

Words and Music by
LYNN DeSHAZO

BEFORE THE THRONE OF GOD ABOVE

Words and Music by VIKKI COOK
and CHARITIE BANCROFT

AT THE CROSS

Words and Music by REUBEN MORGAN
and DARLENE ZSCHECH

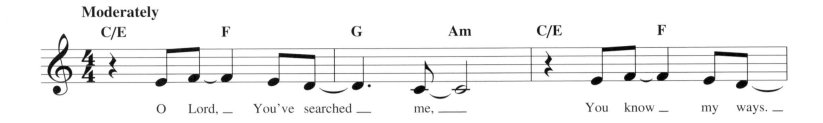

O Lord, __ You've searched __ me, __ You know __ my ways. __

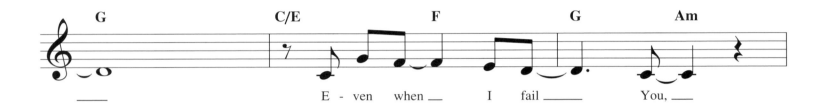

____ E - ven when __ I fail _____ You, ___

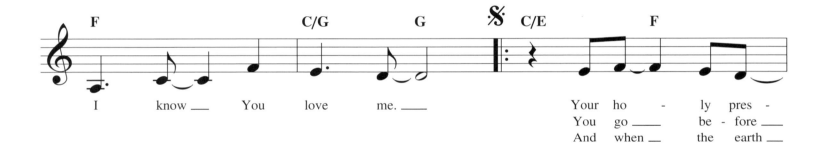

I know __ You love me. ___ Your ho - ly pres -
You go _____ be - fore _____
And when __ the earth __

- ence _____ sur - round - ing me; _____
____ me, _____ You shield __ my way. _____
____ fades, __ falls from __ my eyes, _____

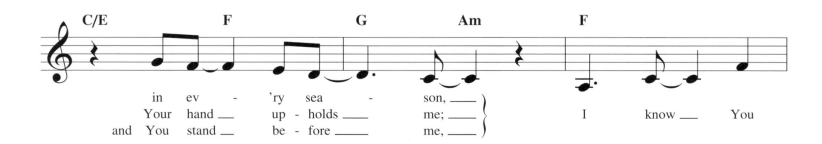

in ev - 'ry sea - son, _____
Your hand __ up - holds _____ me; _____   I know __ You
and You stand __ be - fore _____ me,

AWESOME IS THE LORD MOST HIGH

Words and Music by CHRIS TOMLIN,
JESSE REEVES, CARY PIERCE and JON ABEL

BE GLORIFIED

Words and Music by LOUIE GIGLIO,
CHRIS TOMLIN and JESSE REEVES

With energy

Your love ___ has cap - tured me, ___ Your grace ___ has

set me free; _____ Your life, ___ the air I breathe. ___

Be glo - ri - fied _____ in me. _____

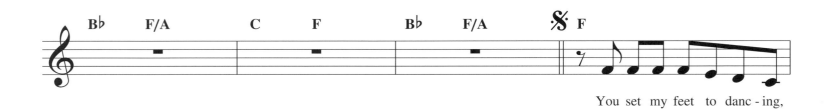

You set my feet to danc - ing,

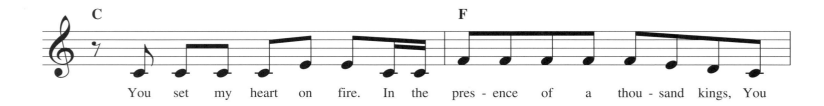

You set my heart on fire. In the pres - ence of a thou - sand kings, You

BEAUTIFUL ONE

Words and Music by
TIM HUGHES

Won - der - ful, so won - der - ful is Your un - fail - ing
Pow - er - ful, so pow - er - ful, Your glo - ry fills the

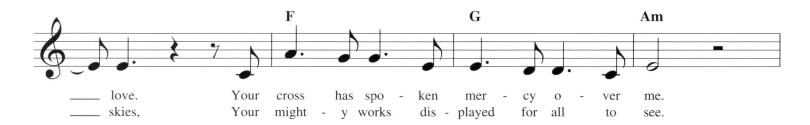

___ love.   Your cross has spo - ken mer - cy o - ver me.
___ skies,   Your might - y works dis - played for all to see.

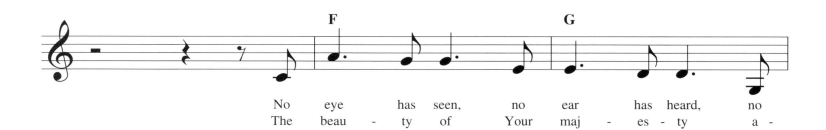

No eye has seen, no ear has heard, no
The beau - ty of Your maj - es - ty a -

heart could ful - ly ___ know   how glo - ri - ous, how
wakes my heart to ___ sing: How mar - vel - ous, how

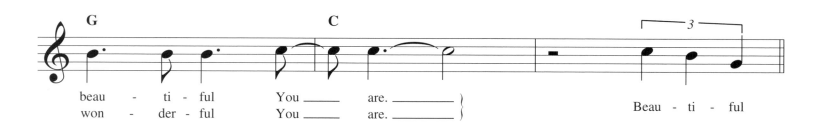

beau - ti - ful You ___ are. ___)
won - der - ful You ___ are. ___)   Beau - ti - ful

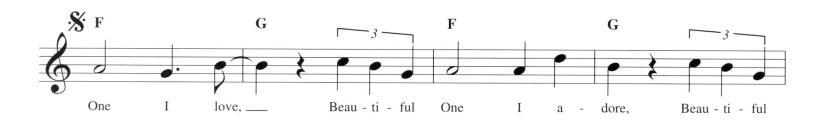

One I love, ___ Beau - ti - ful One I a - dore, Beau - ti - ful

CAME TO MY RESCUE

Words and Music by MARTY SAMPSON,
DYLAN THOMAS and JOEL DAVIES

Moderately

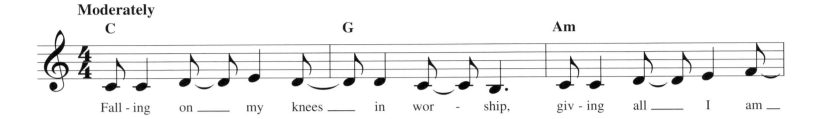

Fall-ing on my knees in wor - ship, giv-ing all I am

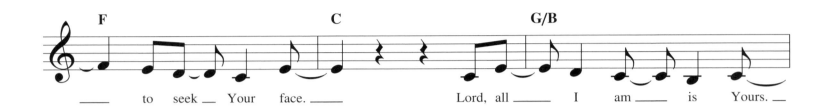

to seek Your face. Lord, all I am is Yours.

My whole life I place

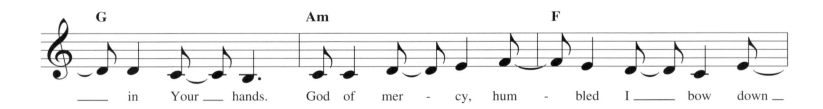

in Your hands. God of mer - cy, hum - bled I bow down

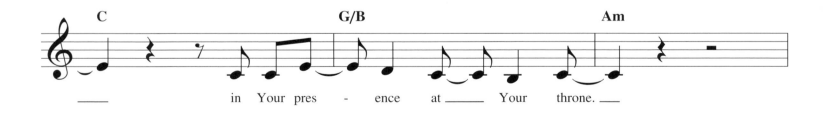

in Your pres - ence at Your throne.

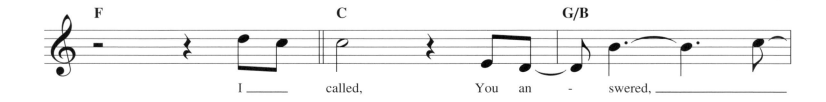

I called, You an - swered,

_____ and You came to my res - cue, and I _____ want to be where _

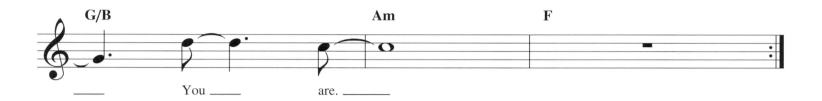

_____ You _____ are. _____

In my life, be lift - ed ____ high. ____ In our world,

be lift - ed ____ high. ____ In our love, be lift - ed ____ high. _

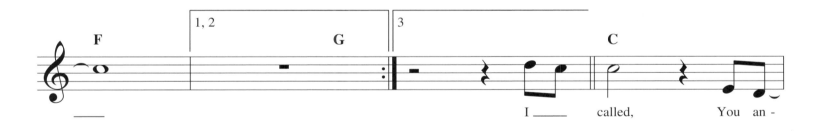

_____ I ____ called, You an -

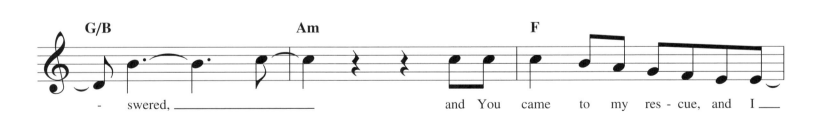

- swered, _____ and You came to my res - cue, and I ___

_____ want to be where ___ You __ are. _____

CENTER

Words and Music by CHARLIE HALL
and MATT REDMAN

Moderately

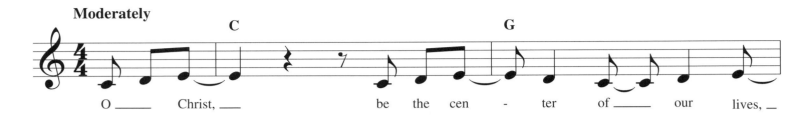

O ___ Christ, ___ be the cen - ter of ___ our lives,

___ be the place ___ we fix ___ our eyes, ___ be the cen -

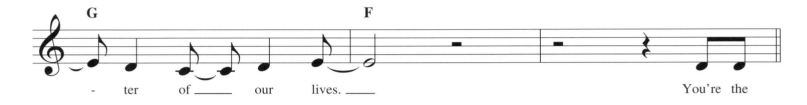

- ter of ___ our lives. ___ You're the

center of the u - ni - verse; ev - 'ry - thing was made in You, ___

Je - sus. ___ Breath of ev - 'ry liv - ing thing, ev - 'ry - one was made for You. _

___ You hold ev - 'ry - thing ___ to - geth - er, You hold ev -

- 'ry - thing ___ to - geth - er. O ___ Christ, _

21

COME THOU FOUNT, COME THOU KING

Traditional
Additional Words and Music by
THOMAS MILLER

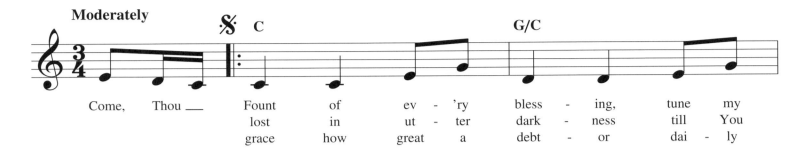

Come, Thou ___ Fount of ev-'ry bless-ing, tune my
lost in ut-ter dark-ness till You
grace how great a debt-or dai-ly

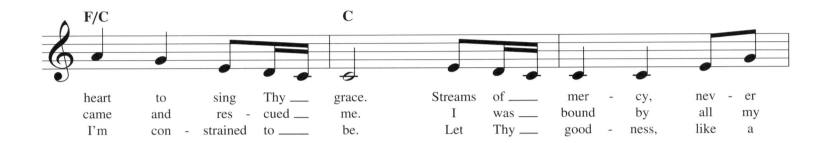

heart to sing Thy ___ grace. Streams of ___ mer-cy, nev-er
came and res-cued ___ me. I was ___ bound by all my
I'm con-strained to ___ be. Let Thy ___ good-ness, like a

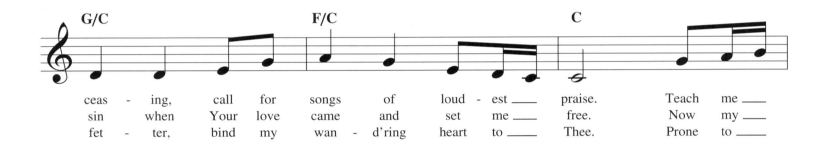

ceas-ing, call for songs of loud-est ___ praise. Teach me ___
sin when Your love came and set me ___ free. Now my ___
fet-ter, bind my wan-d'ring heart to ___ Thee. Prone to ___

some mel-o-dious son-net, sung by ___ flam-ing tongues a-
soul can sing a new ___ song, now my ___ heart has found a
wan-der, Lord, I feel ___ it, prone to ___ leave the God I

bove. Praise the ___ mount, I'm fixed up-on it, mount of
home. Now Your ___ grace is al-ways with me, and I'll
love. Here's my ___ heart, Lord, take and seal it, seal it

COUNTING ON GOD

Words and Music by
JARED ANDERSON

Driving

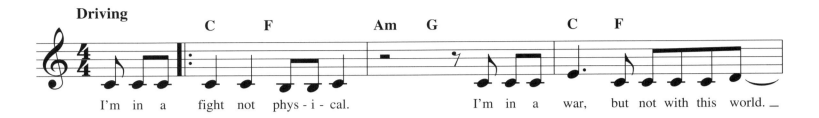

I'm in a fight not phys-i-cal. I'm in a war, but not with this world. ___

___ You are the light that's beau-ti-ful, and I want more, ___

___ I want all ___ that's Yours. ___ Joy un-speak-a-ble that

won't go a-way, ___ and just ___ e-nough strength to live for to-day. ___ So I nev-

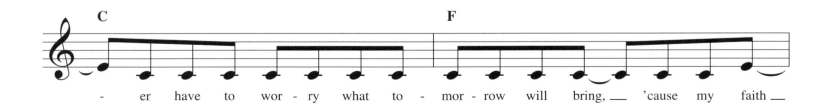

-er have to wor-ry what to-mor-row will bring, ___ 'cause my faith ___

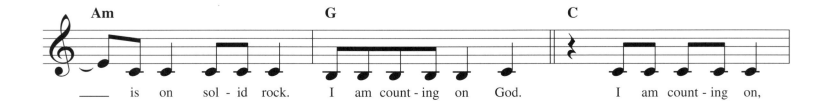

___ is on sol-id rock. I am count-ing on God. I am count-ing on,

DESERT SONG

Words and Music by
BROOKE FRASER

Moderately fast

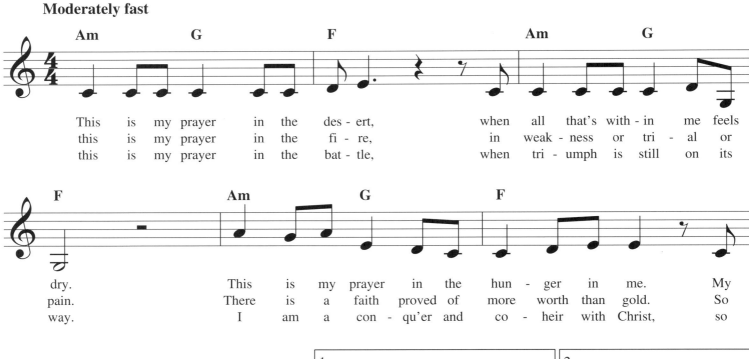

This is my prayer in the des - ert, when all that's with - in me feels
this is my prayer in the fi - re, in weak - ness or tri - al or
this is my prayer in the bat - tle, when tri - umph is still on its

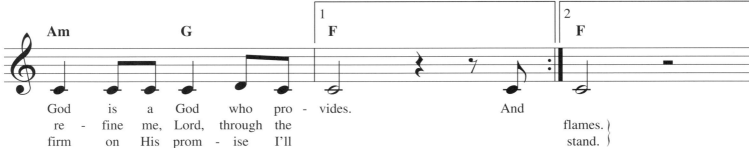

dry. This is my prayer in the hun - ger in me. My
pain. There is a faith proved of more worth than gold. So
way. I am a con - qu'er and co - heir with Christ, so

God is a God who pro - vides. And
re - fine me, Lord, through the flames.
firm on His prom - ise I'll stand.

I will bring praise, I will bring praise. No weap - on formed

a - gainst me shall re - main. I will re - joice, I will de-
clare: God is my vic - to - ry, and He is here.

28

CONSUMING FIRE

Words and Music by
TIM HUGHES

DID YOU FEEL THE MOUNTAINS TREMBLE?

Words and Music by
MARTIN SMITH

Moderately fast

Did you feel the moun-tains trem-ble? __ Did you hear the o - ceans roar

when the peo - ple rose to sing of ___ Je - sus Christ, the Ris - en One? __

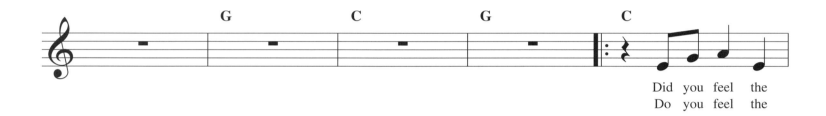

Did you feel the
Do you feel the

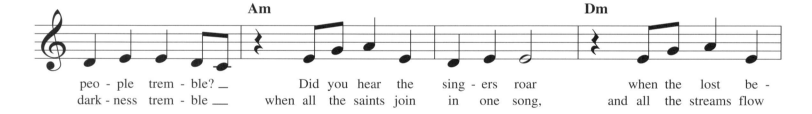

peo - ple trem - ble? __ Did you hear the sing - ers roar when the lost be -
dark - ness trem - ble ___ when all the saints join in one song, and all the streams flow

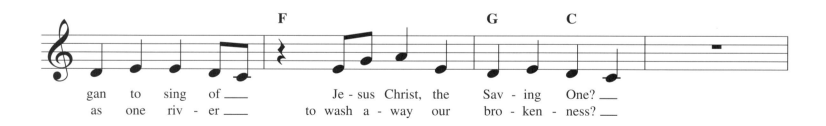

gan to sing of ___ Je - sus Christ, the Sav - ing One? __
as one riv - er ___ to wash a - way our bro - ken - ness?__

And we can see that, God, You're mov - ing, a might - y
And here we see that, God, You're mov - ing; a time of

ENOUGH

Words and Music by CHRIS TOMLIN
and LOUIE GIGLIO

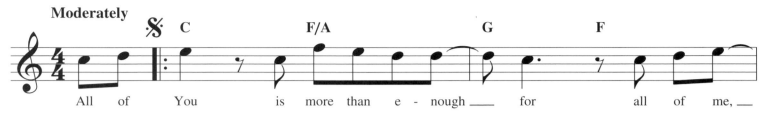

All of You is more than e - nough ___ for all of me, ___

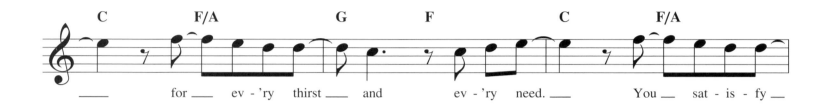

___ for ___ ev - 'ry thirst ___ and ev - 'ry need. ___ You ___ sat - is - fy ___

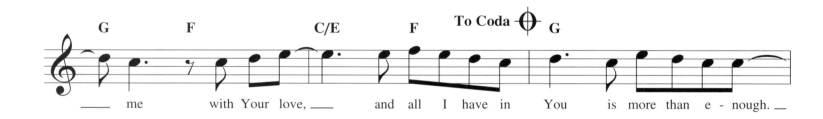

___ me with Your love, ___ and all I have in You is more than e - nough. ___

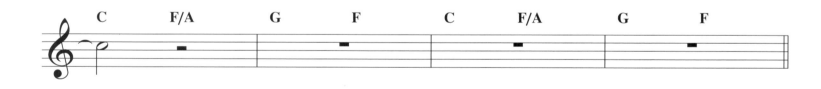

You are my ___ sup - ply, ___ my breath of life, ___ still more awe -
You're my sac - ri - fice ___ of great - est price, ___ still more awe -

- some than I know. You are my ___ re - ward, ___ worth liv - ing for, ___
- some than I know. You're my com - ing King, ___ You are ev - 'ry - thing, ___

EVERYDAY

Words and Music by
JOEL HOUSTON

Moderately, fast groove

What to say, Lord? It's ___ You who gave me life, and I can't ex-plain just how ___

___ much You mean to me now ___ that You have saved me, Lord. ___ I give all that I am to

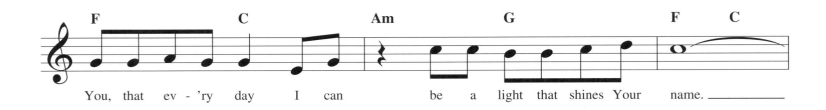

You, that ev-'ry day I can be a light that shines Your name. ___

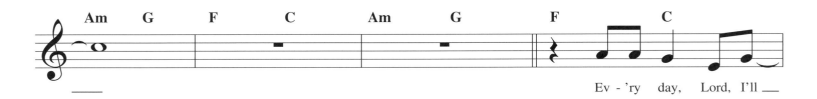

___ Ev-'ry day, Lord, I'll ___

___ learn to stand up-on Your Word. And I pray that I, ___ that I may come to know You

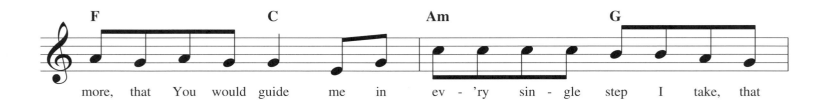

more, that You would guide me in ev-'ry sin-gle step I take, that

ev-'ry day I can be Your Light un-to the

FAMOUS ONE

Words and Music by CHRIS TOMLIN
and JESSE REEVES

FOR ALL YOU'VE DONE

Words and Music by
REUBEN MORGAN

FOR WHO YOU ARE

Words and Music by
MARTY SAMPSON

Moderately

Stand - ing here   in Your pres - ence,   think - ing of the good __

__ things You __ have done. __ Wait - ing here   pa - tient - ly,

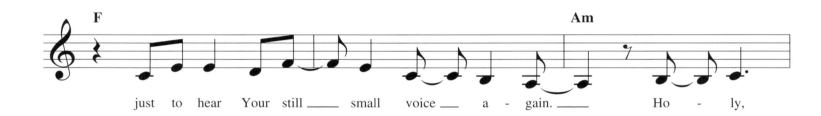

just to hear Your still __ small voice __ a - gain. __   Ho - ly,

right - eous,   faith - ful till __ the end. __

Sav - ior,   Heal - er, Re - deem - er __ and Friend. __

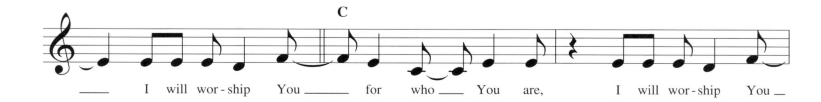

__ I will wor - ship You __ for who __ You are,   I will wor - ship You __

39

FRIEND OF GOD

Words and Music by MICHAEL GUNGOR
and ISRAEL HOUGHTON

Moderately fast

Who am I ____ that You ____ are mind - ful ____ of ____ me,

that ____ You ____ hear ____ me   when ___ I   call? ____

____   Is   it   true ____   that   You ___

____ are think - ing ___ of ____ me?   How ___ You ___ love ___

____ me;   it's a - maz - ing! ____

I am a friend ___ of God, ____   I am a friend ___ of God, ___

FROM THE INSIDE OUT

Words and Music by
JOEL HOUSTON

A thou-sand times I've failed, __ still Your mer - cy re - mains. __ And should I

bove all else, __ my pur - pose re - mains, __ the art of

stum - ble a - gain, __ I'm caught __ in Your grace. }
los - ing my - self __ in bring - ing You praise. } Ev - er - last - ing, Your light will shine when

all else fades. Nev - er - end - ing, Your glo - ry goes be - yond all fame.

(Instrumental)

Your will, a -

yond all fame.   In my heart and my soul, __   I give You con - trol. __

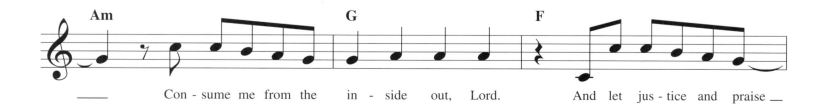

__ Con - sume me from the in - side out, Lord.   And let jus - tice and praise __

GIVE US CLEAN HANDS

Words and Music by
CHARLIE HALL

FOREVER REIGN

Words and Music by REUBEN MORGAN
and JASON INGRAM

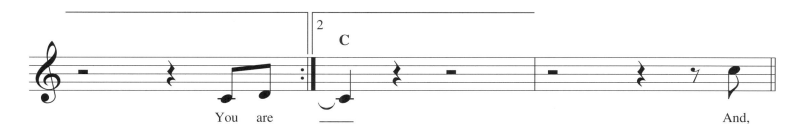

love will al - ways be e - nough. Noth - ing com - pares ___ to Your ___ em - brace. ___

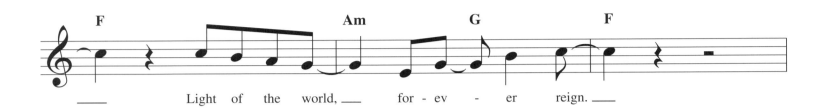

___ Light of the world, ___ for - ev - er reign. ___

You are more, You are more than my words will ev - er say. You are

Lord, You are Lord, all cre - a - tion will pro - claim. You are here, You are here; in Your

pres - ence I'm made whole. You are God, You are God; of all else I'm let - ting go. ___

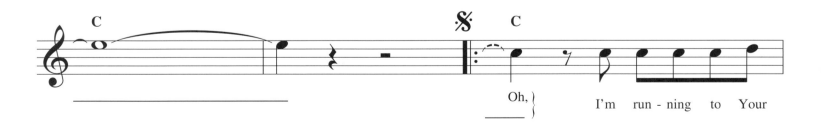

___ Oh, I'm run - ning to Your

arms, I'm run - ning to Your arms. The rich - es of Your love will al - ways be e -

GLORY IN THE HIGHEST

Words and Music by CHRIS TOMLIN, JESSE REEVES,
DANIEL CARSON, MATT REDMAN and ED CASH

Moderately

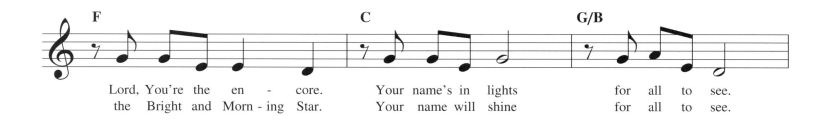

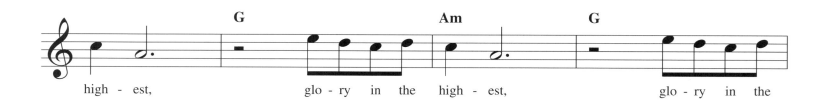

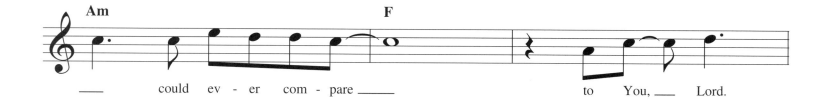

GLORY TO GOD FOREVER

Words and Music by STEVE FEE
and VICKY BEECHING

Grace Flows Down

Words and Music by LOUIE GIGLIO,
DAVID BELL and ROD PADGETT

GOD IS GREAT

Words and Music by
MARTY SAMPSON

GOD OF THIS CITY

Words and Music by AARON BOYD,
PETER COMFORT, RICHARD BLEAKLEY,
PETER KERNAGHAN, ANDREW McCANN
and IAN JORDAN

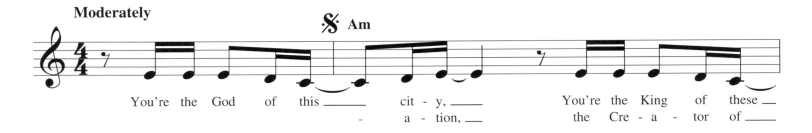

You're the God of this city, You're the King of these na - tion, the Cre - a - tor of

peo - ple, You're the Lord of this na - tion, You are.
all things, You're the King a - bove all kings, You are.

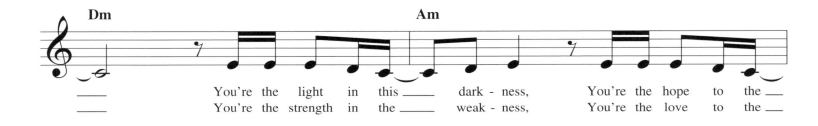

You're the light in this dark - ness, You're the hope to the
You're the strength in the weak - ness, You're the love to the

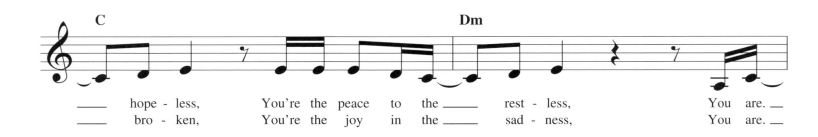

hope - less, You're the peace to the rest - less, You are.
bro - ken, You're the joy in the sad - ness, You are.

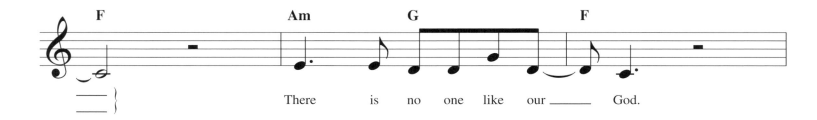

There is no one like our God.

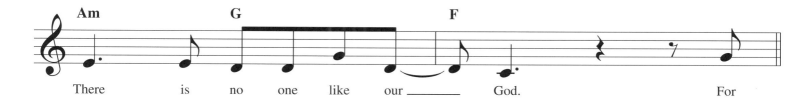

There is no one like our _____ God. For

great - er things have yet to come, and great - er things are still to be done in this __

__ cit - y. _____

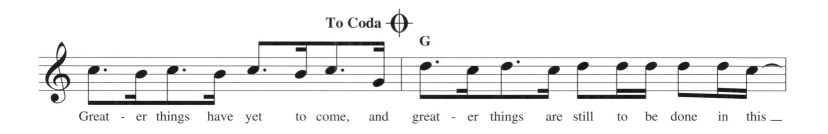

To Coda

Great - er things have yet to come, and great - er things are still to be done in this __

D.S. al Coda

__ cit - y. _____ You're the Lord of cre -

CODA

great - er things are still to be done here. _____

HAPPY DAY

Words and Music by TIM HUGHES
and BEN CANTELLON

57

HEALER

Words and Music by
MIKE GUGLIELMUCCI

You hold my ev - 'ry mo - ment, You calm my rag - ing seas. __

__ You walk with me __ through fi - re and

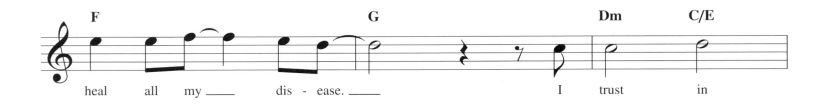

heal all my __ dis - ease. __ I trust in

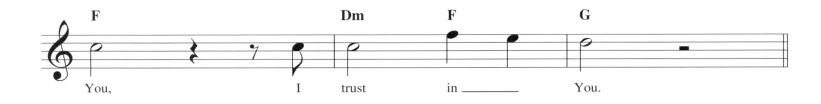

You, I trust in _____ You.

I be - lieve You're my heal - er. I be - lieve

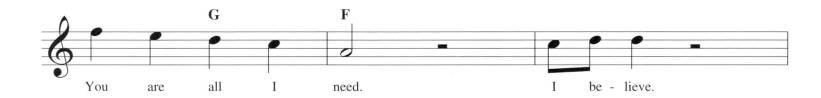

You are all I need. I be - lieve.

60

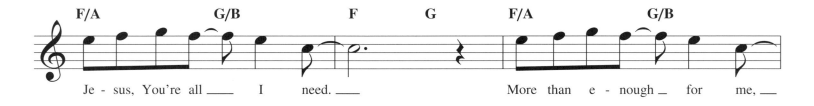

HEAR US FROM HEAVEN

Words and Music by
JARED ANDERSON

Moderately

Lord, hear our cry, _____ come heal our land. _____
Lord, hear our prayer, _____ for-give our sins. _____
Lord, hear our song, _____ Your chil-dren wor-ship.

Breathe life in-to these _____ dry and thirst-y _____ souls. _____
As we call on Your name, _____ would You make _____ this a place _____
As we sing out Your praise, _____ would You make _____ this a place _____

_____ for Your glo - ry to dwell? _____ }
_____ for Your glo - ry to dwell? _____ }

O - pen the blind _____ eyes, un-lock the deaf _____ _____ ears, come to Your peo - ple as we draw near. _____ Hear us from heav-

-en, touch our gen-er-a - tion. We are Your peo - ple, cry-ing out _____ in

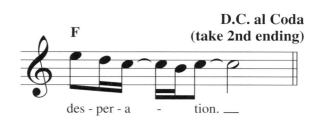

**D.C. al Coda
(take 2nd ending)**

des - per - a - tion. _____

CODA

des - per - a - tion. _____

HERE IN YOUR PRESENCE

Words and Music by
JON EGAN

Slowly, in 2

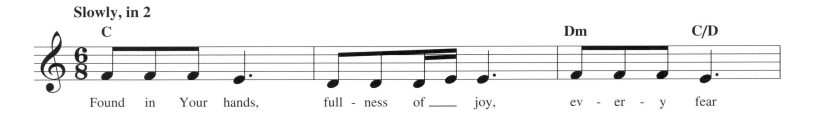

Found in Your hands, full - ness of ___ joy, ev - er - y fear

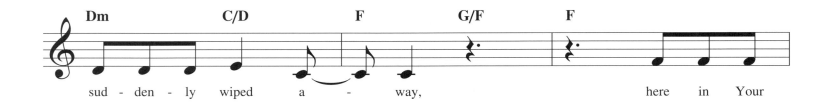

sud - den - ly wiped a - way, here in Your

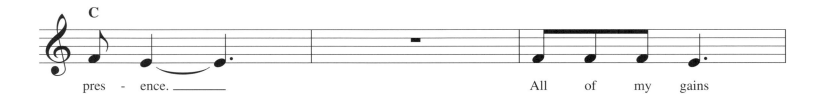

pres - ence. _____ All of my gains

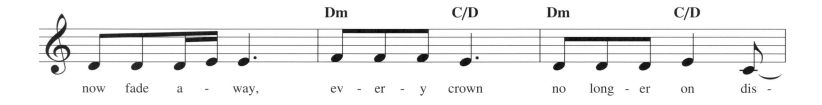

now fade a - way, ev - er - y crown no long - er on dis -

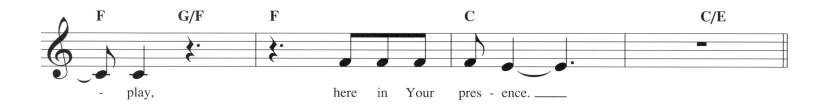

- play, here in Your pres - ence. _____

Heav - en is trem - bling in awe of Your won - ders, _____

HOSANNA

Words and Music by
BROOKE FRASER

Moderately

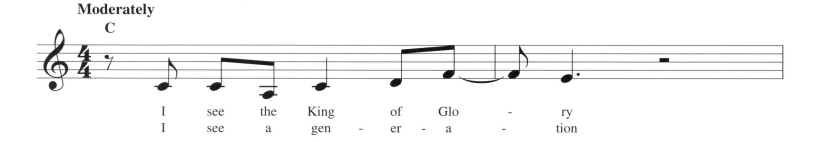

I see the King of Glo - ry
I see a gen - er - a - tion

com - ing on the clouds with fire. _____ The whole earth shakes, _____
ris - ing up to take with their place _____ with self - less faith, _____

_____ the whole earth shakes. _____ I see His love and mer -
_____ with self - less faith. _____ I see a near re - viv -

- cy _____ wash - ing o - ver all our sin. _____ The peo - ple sing, _____
- al _____ stir - ring as we pray and seek. _____ We're on our knees, _____

_____ the peo - ple sing. _____)
_____ we're on our knees. _____ }   Ho - san -

- na, _____ ho - san - na, _____ ho - san - na in the high - est. _____

HOSANNA
(Praise Is Rising)

Words and Music by PAUL BALOCHE
and BRENTON BROWN

Brightly

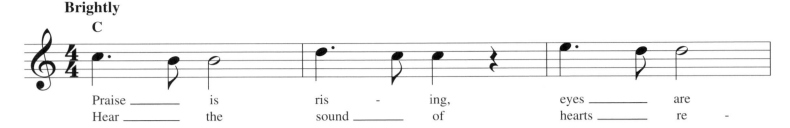

Praise _____ is ris - ing, eyes _____ are
Hear _____ the sound _____ of hearts _____ re -

turn - ing _____ to You. _____ We turn to You. _____
turn - ing _____ to You. _____ We turn to You. _____

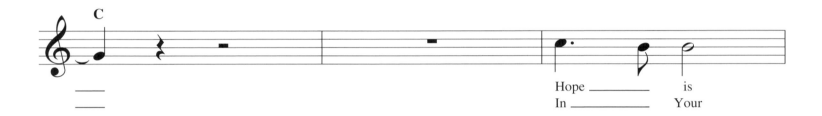

_____
_____ Hope _____ is
In _____ Your

stir - ring, hearts _____ are yearn - ing _____ for You. _____
King - dom, bro - ken lives are _____ made new. _____

_____ We long for You. _____ }
_____ You make us new. _____ }

'Cause when we see _____ You, we find strength _ to face the day. _____

HOW CAN I KEEP FROM SINGING

Words and Music by CHRIS TOMLIN,
MATT REDMAN and ED CASH

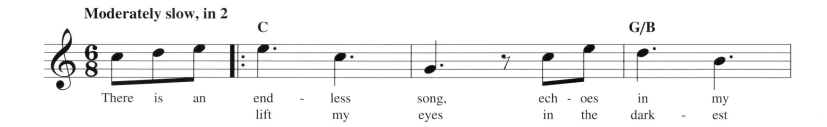

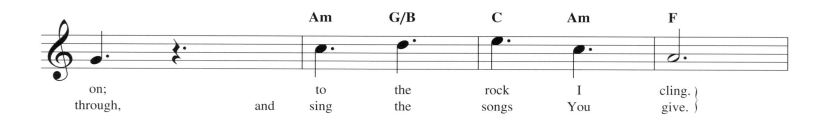

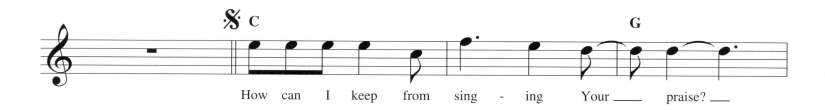

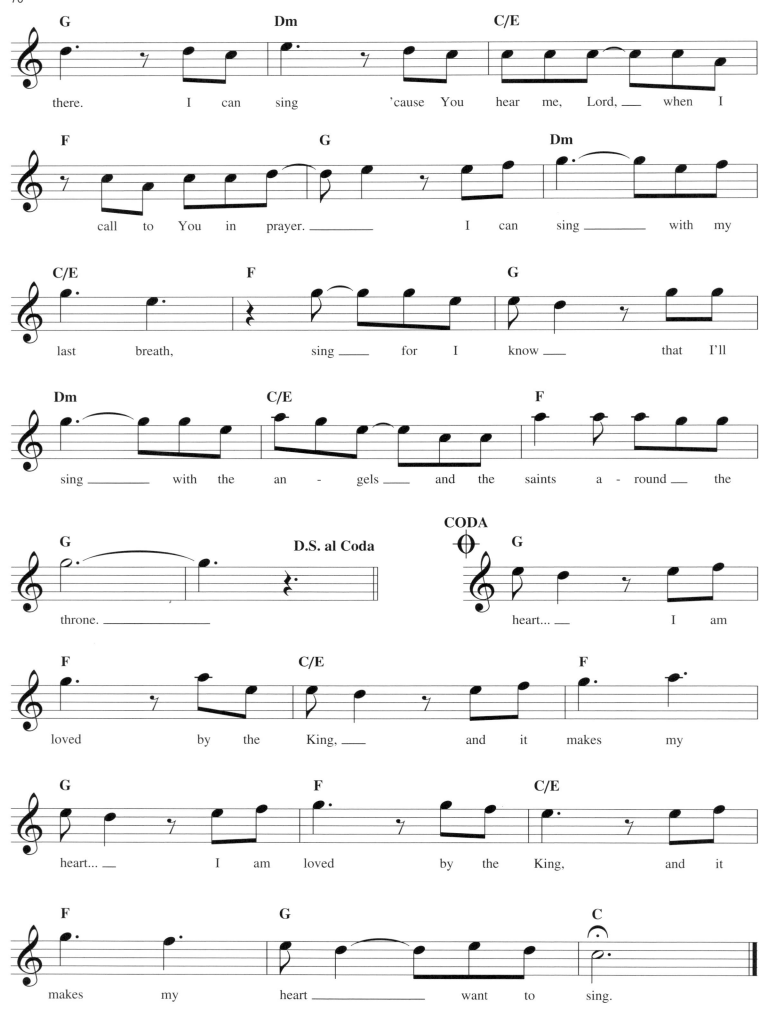

HOW DEEP THE FATHER'S LOVE FOR US

Words and Music by
STUART TOWNEND

Reflectively

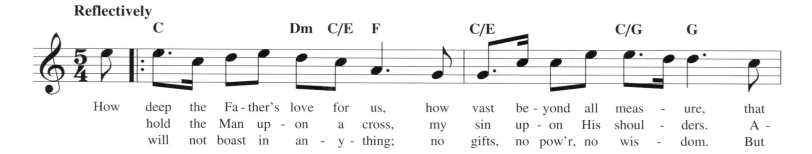

How deep the Fa-ther's love for us, how vast be-yond all meas-ure, that
hold the Man up-on a cross, my sin up-on His shoul-ders. A-
will not boast in an-y-thing; no gifts, no pow'r, no wis-dom. But

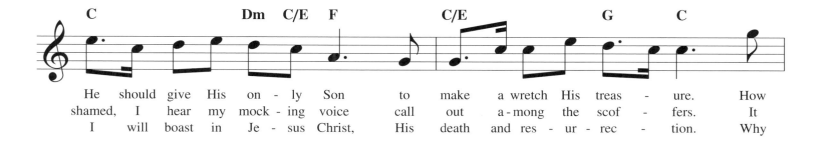

He should give His on-ly Son to make a wretch His treas-ure. How
shamed, I hear my mock-ing voice call out a-mong the scof-fers. It
I will boast in Je-sus Christ, His death and res-ur-rec-tion. Why

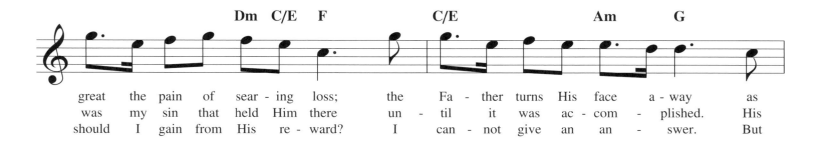

great the pain of sear-ing loss; the Fa-ther turns His face a-way as
was my sin that held Him there un-til it was ac-com-plished. His
should I gain from His re-ward? I can-not give an an-swer. But

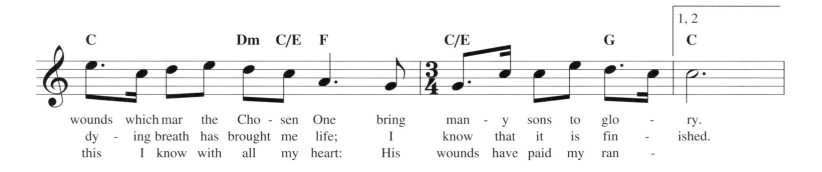

wounds which mar the Cho-sen One bring man-y sons to glo-ry.
dy-ing breath has brought me life; I know that it is fin-ished.
this I know with all my heart: His wounds have paid my ran-

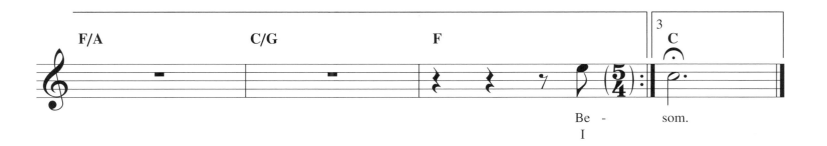

Be-som.
I

HOW GREAT IS OUR GOD

Words and Music by CHRIS TOMLIN,
JESSE REEVES and ED CASH

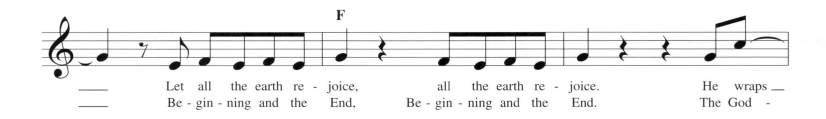

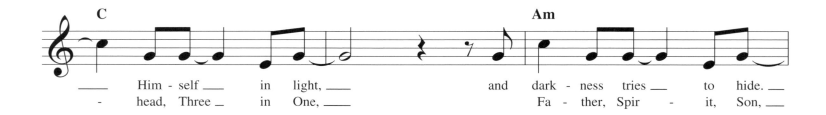

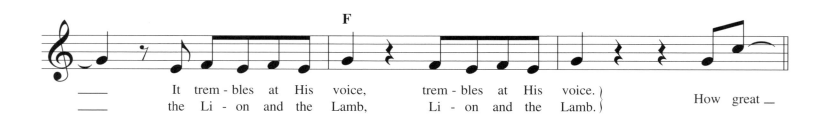

HOW HE LOVES

Words and Music by
JOHN MARK McMILLAN

I AM FREE

Words and Music by
JON EGAN

I WILL BOAST

Words and Music by
PAUL BALOCHE

JESUS MESSIAH

Words and Music by CHRIS TOMLIN,
JESSE REEVES, DANIEL CARSON
and ED CASH

He be-came sin, who knew no sin, that
bod-y the bread, His blood the wine,

we might be-come His right-eous-ness. He
bro-ken and poured out all for love. The

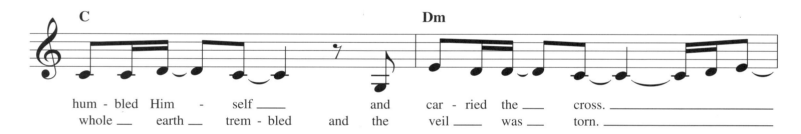

hum-bled Him-self and car-ried the cross.
whole earth trem-bled and the veil was torn.

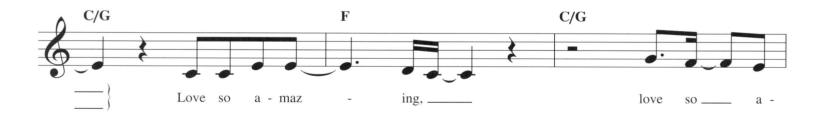

Love so a-maz-ing, love so a-

maz-ing. Je-sus, Mes-si-ah,

Name a-bove all names, Bless-ed Re-deem-er,

LEAD ME TO THE CROSS

Words and Music by
BROOKE FRASER

Moderately slow

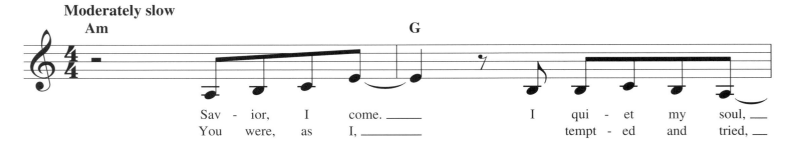

Sav - ior, I come. ____ I qui - et my soul, ____
You were, as I, _____ tempt - ed and tried, ____

____ re - mem - ber ____ re - demp - tion's hill ____
____ hu - man. ____ Word be - came flesh, ____

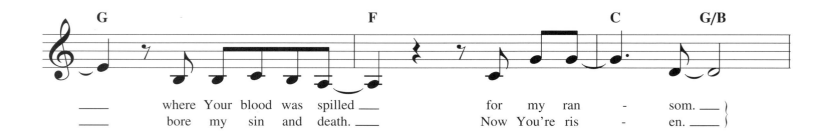

____ where Your blood was spilled ____ for my ran - som. ____)
____ bore my sin and death. ____ Now You're ris - en. ____)

And ev - 'ry - thing ____ I once held dear, ____ I count ____

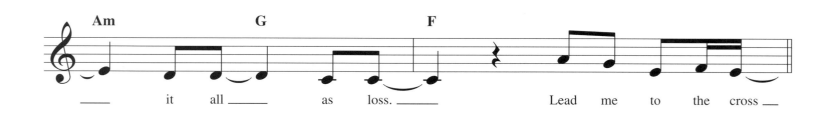

____ it all ____ as loss. ____ Lead me to the cross ____

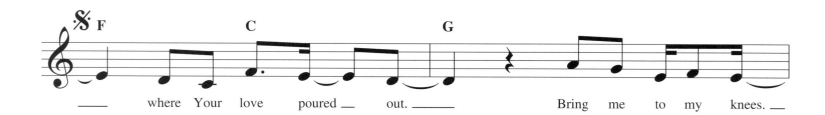

____ where Your love poured ____ out. ____ Bring me to my knees. ____

LET EVERYTHING THAT HAS BREATH

Words and Music by
MATT REDMAN

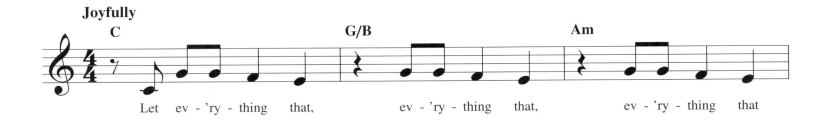

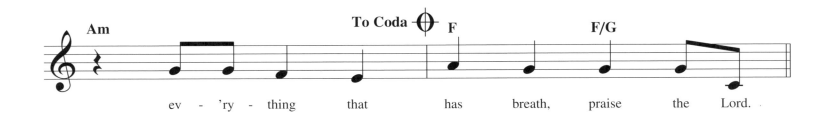

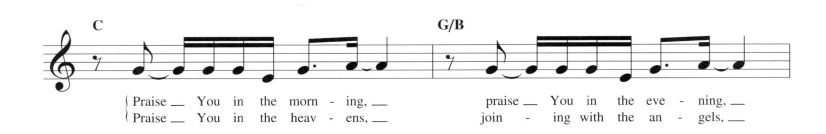

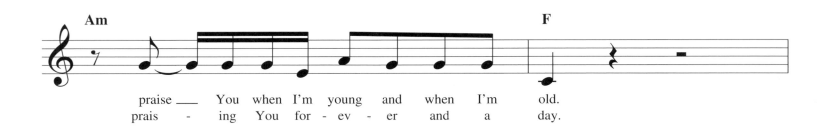

83

Praise — You when I'm laugh - ing, ___ praise — You when I'm griev - ing, ___
Praise — You on the earth now, ___ join - ing with cre - a - tion, ___

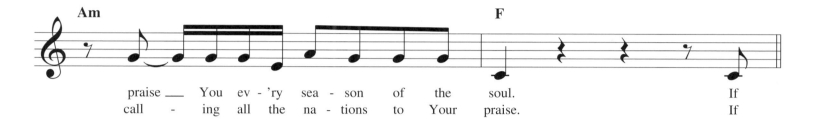

praise ___ You ev - 'ry sea - son of the soul. If
call - ing all the na - tions to Your praise. If

we } could see how much You're worth, Your pow'r, Your might, Your
they }

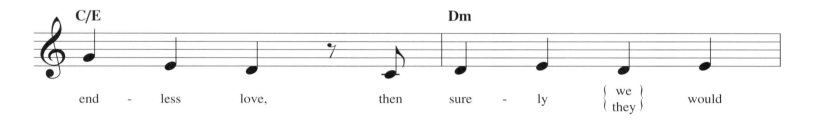

end - less love, then sure - ly { we } would
{ they }

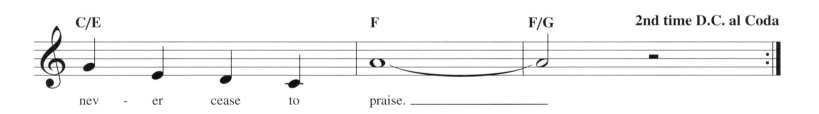

2nd time D.C. al Coda

nev - er cease to praise. ___

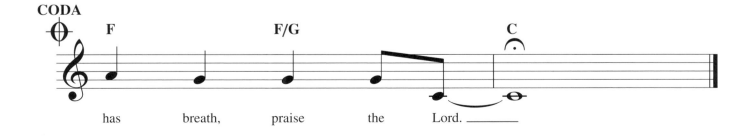

CODA

has breath, praise the Lord. ___

LET GOD ARISE

Words and Music by CHRIS TOMLIN,
JESSE REEVES and ED CASH

JESUS SAVES

Words and Music by TIM HUGHES
and NICK HERBERT

With energy

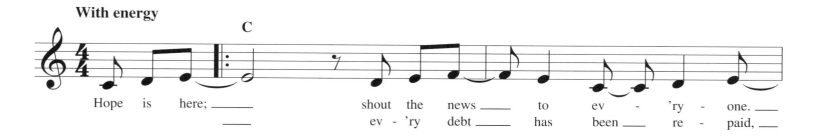

Hope is here; _____ shout the news _____ to ev - 'ry - one. _____
_____ ev - 'ry debt _____ has been _____ re - paid,

_____ It's a new _____ day, peace _____ has come. _____
_____ bro - ken hearts _____ can be _____ re - made.

Je - sus _____ saves. _____ Mer - cy tri - umphs at _____ the cross,
Je - sus _____ saves. _____ Sing a - bove _____ the storms _____ of life,

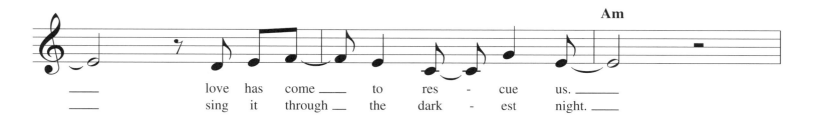

_____ love has come _____ to res - cue us. _____
_____ sing it through _____ the dark - est night. _____

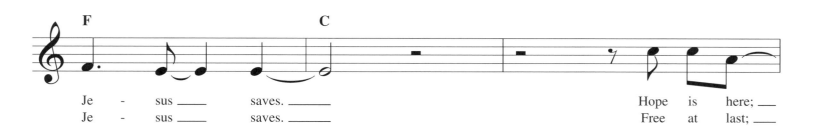

Je - sus _____ saves. _____ Hope is here; _____
Je - sus _____ saves. _____ Free at last; _____

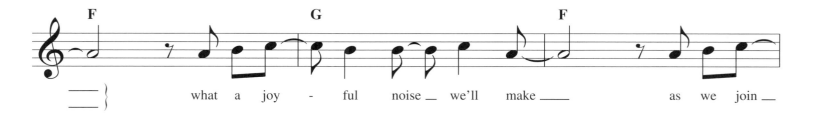

_____ what a joy - ful noise _ we'll make _____ as we join _____

LET IT RISE

Words and Music by
HOLLAND DAVIS

Let the glo - ry of ___ the Lord ___ rise a - mong ___ us. Let the
songs ___ of ___ the Lord ___ rise a - mong ___ us. Let the

glo - ry of ___ the Lord ___ rise a - mong ___ us. Let the
songs ___ of ___ the Lord ___ rise a - mong ___ us. Let the

prais - es of ___ the King ___ rise a - mong ___ us, let it rise. ___
joy ___ of ___ the King ___ rise a - mong ___ us, let it rise. ___

___   Let the   Oh, _____

___   let it rise. ___   Oh, _____

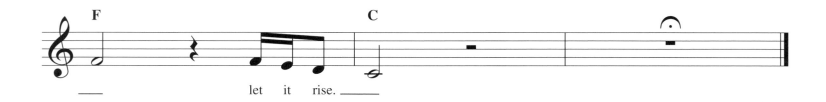

___   let it rise. _____

LET MY WORDS BE FEW
(I'll Stand in Awe of You)

Words and Music by MATT REDMAN
and BETH REDMAN

LET THE PRAISES RING

Words and Music by
LINCOLN BREWSTER

Joyfully

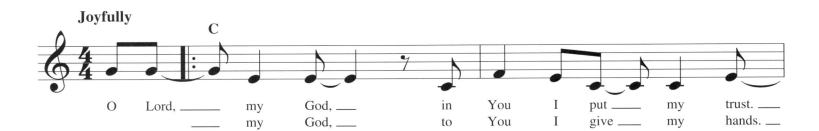

O Lord, ___ my God, ___ in You I put ___ my trust. ___
___ my God, ___ to You I give ___ my hands. ___

___ O Lord, ___ my God, ___ in
___ O Lord, ___ my God, ___ to

You I put ___ my hope. ___   O Lord, ___
You I give ___ my feet. ___   O Lord, ___

___ my God, ___ in You I put ___ my trust, ___ oh ___ yes, I do. ___
___ my God, ___ to You I give ___ my ev - 'ry - thing. Take ___ all I am. ___

___ O Lord, ___ my God, ___ in You I put ___ my ___
___ O Lord, ___ my God, ___ to You I give ___ my ___

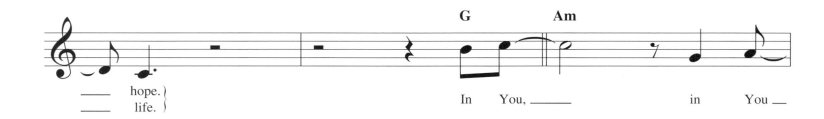

___ hope.)
___ life.)   In You, _____ in You ___

I find ___ my peace. ___ In You, ___

___ in You ___ I find ___ my strength. ___

In You ___ I live ___ and move ___ and breathe. ___

___ Let ev - 'ry - thing ___ I say and do ___ be

found - ed by ___ my faith in You. ___ I lift up ho - ly hands and sing.

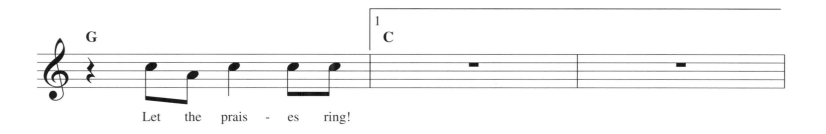

Let the prais - es ring!

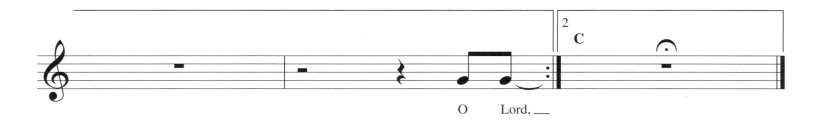

O Lord, ___

THE LORD REIGNS

Words and Music by
KLAUS KUEHN

With excitement

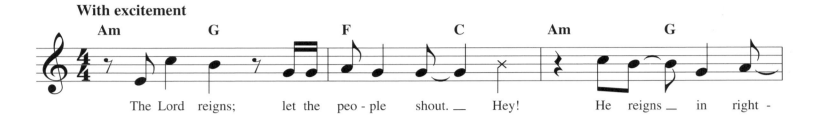

The Lord reigns; let the peo - ple shout. __ Hey! He reigns __ in right -

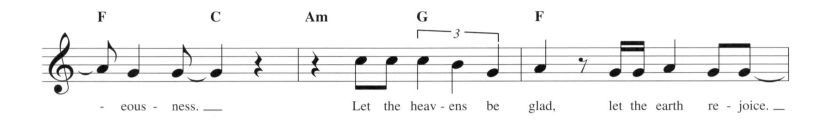

- eous - ness. __ Let the heav - ens be glad, let the earth re - joice. __

__ The Lord reigns; let the

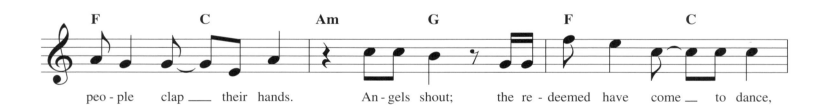

peo - ple clap __ their hands. An - gels shout; the re - deemed have come __ to dance,

to cel - e - brate, to cel - e - brate. He reigns! _____

The Lord reigns, the Lord reigns, the Lord reigns.

93

MADE ME GLAD

Words and Music by
MIRIAM WEBSTER

LOVE THE LORD

Words and Music by
LINCOLN BREWSTER

Love the Lord your God with all your heart, with all your soul, with all your
I will serve the Lord with all my heart, with all my soul, with all my
I will love You, Lord, with all my heart, with all my soul, with all my

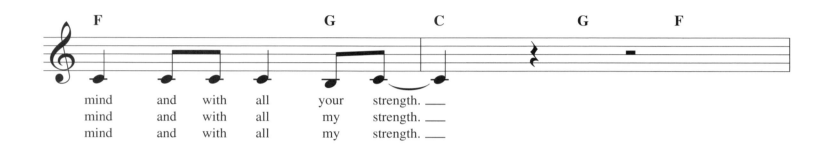

mind and with all your strength. ___
mind and with all my strength. ___
mind and with all my strength. ___

Love the Lord your God with all your heart, with all your soul, with all your
I will serve the Lord with all my heart, with all my soul, with all my
I will love You, Lord, with all my heart, with all my soul, with all my

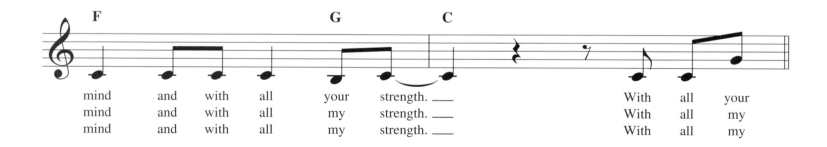

mind and with all your strength. ___ With all your
mind and with all my strength. ___ With all my
mind and with all my strength. ___ With all my

heart, _____ with all your soul, with all your
heart, _____ with all my soul, with all my
heart, _____ with all my soul, with all my

mind, _____ with all your strength.
mind, _____ with all my strength.
mind, _____ with all my strength.

Love the Lord your God with all your heart, with all your soul, with all your
I will serve the Lord with all my heart, with all my soul, with all my
I will love You, Lord, with all my heart, with all my soul, with all my

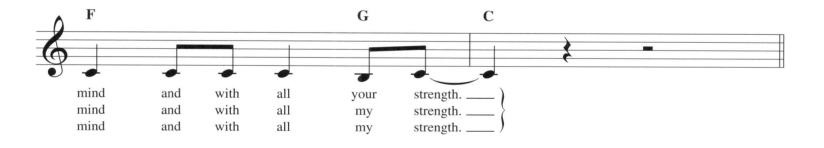

mind and with all your strength. _____
mind and with all my strength. _____
mind and with all my strength. _____

Da da dum, da da dum da da dah. _____ Da da dum, da da dum da da dah. _____

Repeat twice

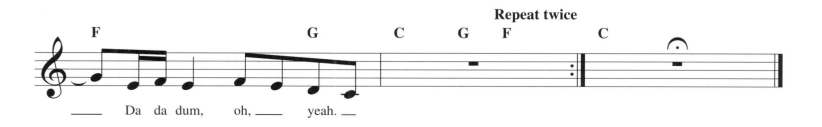

_____ Da da dum, oh, _____ yeah. _____

MADE TO WORSHIP

Words and Music by CHRIS TOMLIN,
ED CASH and STEPHAN SHARP

Be - fore the day, ___ be - fore the light, ___ be - i-
All we are ___ and all we have ___ is

fore the world ___ re - volved a - round ___ the sun,
all a gift ___ from God that we ___ re - ceive.

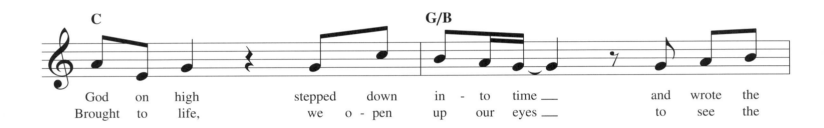

God on high stepped down in - to time ___ and wrote the
Brought to life, we o - pen up our eyes ___ to see the

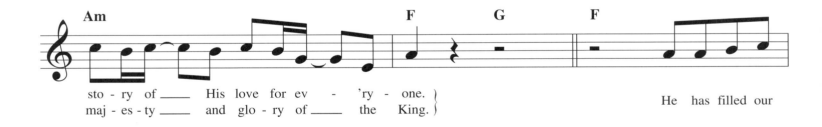

sto - ry of ___ His love for ev - 'ry - one. }
maj - es - ty ___ and glo - ry of ___ the King. }   He has filled our

hearts with won - der so that we al - ways re - mem - ber: ___

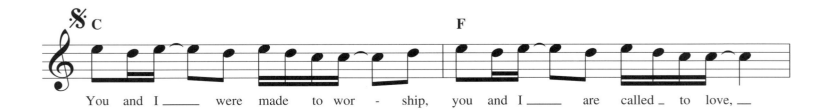

You and I ___ were made to wor - ship, you and I ___ are called _ to love, ___

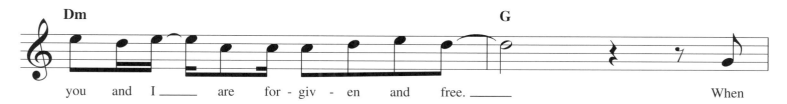

you and I ____ are for - giv - en and free. _____ When

you and I ____ em - brace, sur - ren - der, you and I ____ choose to ____ be - lieve, ____ then

you and I will see _____ who we were meant ___ to be.

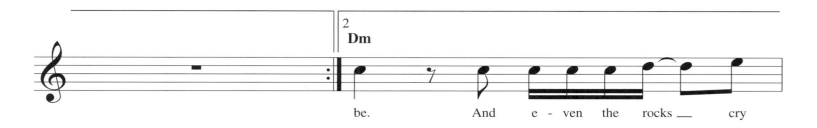

be. And e - ven the rocks ___ cry

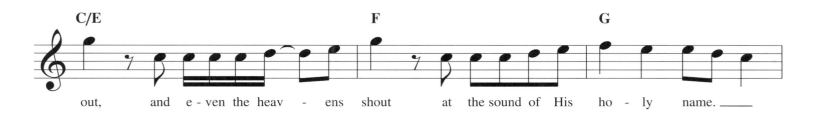

out, and e - ven the heav - ens shout at the sound of His ho - ly name. ____

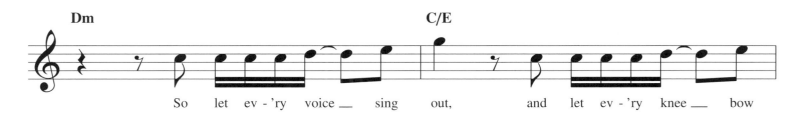

So let ev - 'ry voice ___ sing out, and let ev - 'ry knee ___ bow

down; He is wor - thy of all our praise. ____ be.

MAJESTIC

Words and Music by
LINCOLN BREWSTER

High energy

O   Lord,   our __ Lord, __ how ma - jes - tic __ is __ Your   name __

__ in all __ the earth. _____ O   Lord,   our __ Lord, __ how ma -

jes - tic __ is __ Your name ___ in all __ the earth. ___ The heav - ens __ de -

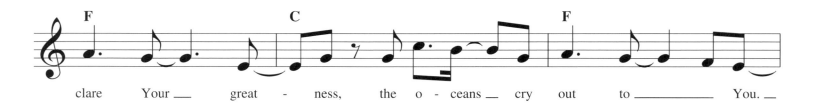

clare Your __ great - ness,   the o - ceans __ cry   out   to ___ You. __

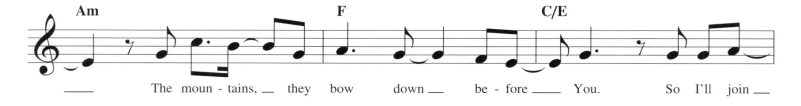

__ The moun - tains, __ they   bow   down __ be - fore __ You.   So I'll   join __

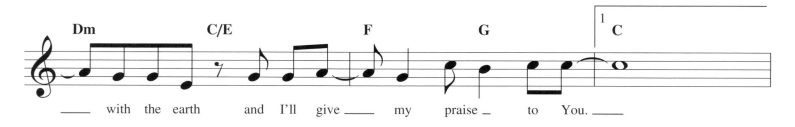

__ with   the   earth   and   I'll   give __ my   praise __ to   You. ___

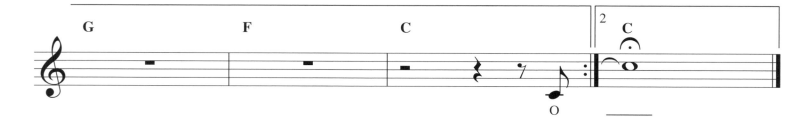

O ___

NEW DOXOLOGY

Original Words and Music by GENEVAN PSALTER and THOMAS KEN
New Lyrics and Chorus by THOMAS MILLER

MAJESTY
(Here I Am)

Words and Music by MARTIN SMITH
and STUART GARRARD

Moderately slow

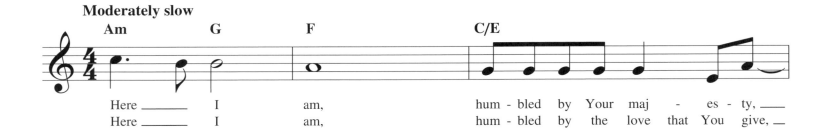

Here _____ I am, hum - bled by Your maj - es - ty, _____
Here _____ I am, hum - bled by the love that You give, _

_____ cov - ered by Your grace so _____ free. _____
_____ for - giv - en so that I can for - give. _____

Here _____ I am, know - ing I'm a sin - ful man, _
Here _____ I stand, know - ing I am Your de - sire, _

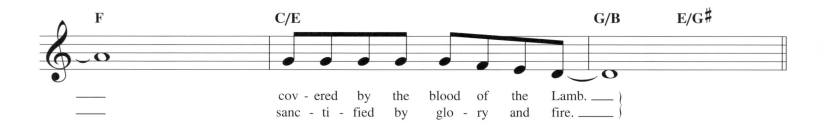

_____ cov - ered by the blood of the Lamb. _____
_____ sanc - ti - fied by glo - ry and fire. _____

Now I've found the great - est love of all is

103

mine   since   You   laid   down   Your   life,   the   great - est   sac - ri -

fice.   Sing - in':   Maj   -   es - ty, ___

___   maj   -   es - ty. ___   {(1., 2.) Your (3.) For -

grace   has   found   me   just   as   I   am, ___   emp - ty -
ev - er   I   am   changed   by   Your   love ___   in   the

hand - ed,   but   a - live   in   Your   hands. ___   ___   Sing - in':

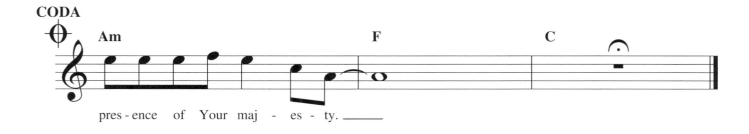

pres - ence   of   Your   maj   -   es - ty. ___

MARVELOUS LIGHT

Words and Music by
CHARLIE HALL

MIGHTY TO SAVE

Words and Music by BEN FIELDING
and REUBEN MORGAN

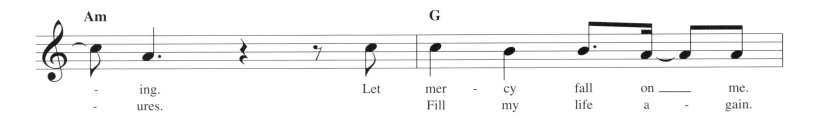

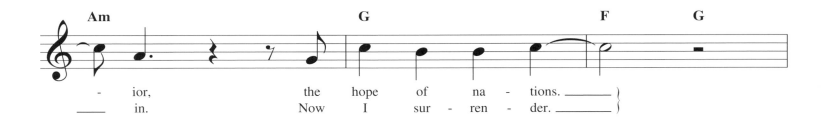

MY SAVIOR LIVES

Words and Music by JON EGAN
and GLENN PACKIAM

High energy

Our God will reign _____ for - ev - er, and all the world _____
The King has come _____ from heav - en, and dark - ness trem -

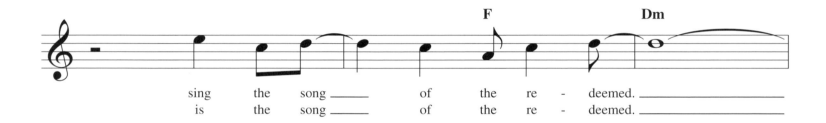

_____ will know His name. _____ Ev - 'ry - one _____ to - geth - er,
- bles at His name. _____ Vic - to - ry _____ for - ev - er

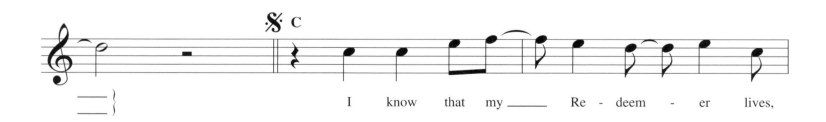

sing the song _____ of the re - deemed. _____
is the song _____ of the re - deemed. _____

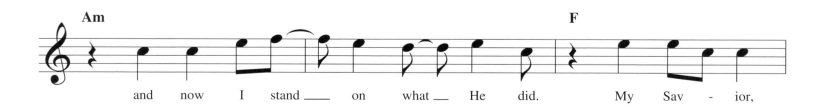

I know that my _____ Re - deem - er lives,

and now I stand _____ on what _____ He did. My Sav - ior,

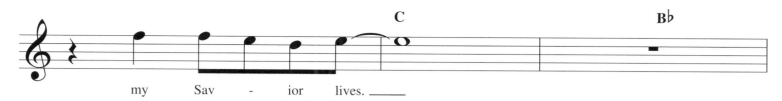

my Sav - ior lives. _____

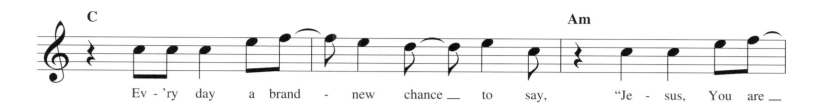

Ev - 'ry day a brand - new chance _ to say, "Je - sus, You are _

_ the on - ly way." My Sav - ior, my Sav - ior lives. _

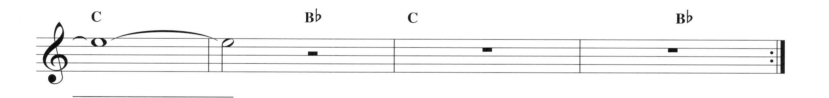

My Sav - ior lives, my

Sav - ior lives, my Sav - ior

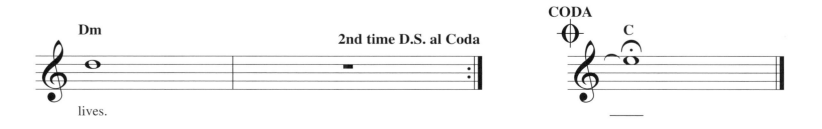

lives.

A NEW HALLELUJAH

Words and Music by PAUL BALOCHE,
MICHAEL W. SMITH and DEBBIE SMITH

Moderately fast

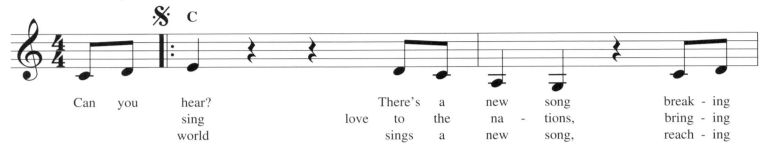

Can you hear? There's a new song break-ing
sing love to the na - tions, bring-ing
world sings a new song, reach-ing

out from the chil - dren of free - dom. Ev - 'ry
hope of the grace that has freed ___ us. Make it
out with a new hal - le - lu - jah. Ev - 'ry

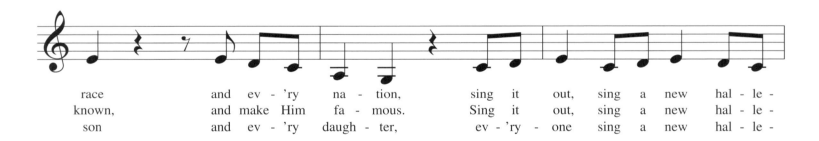

race and ev - 'ry na - tion, sing it out, sing a new hal - le -
known, and make Him fa - mous. Sing it out, sing a new hal - le -
son and ev - 'ry daugh - ter, ev - 'ry - one sing a new hal - le -

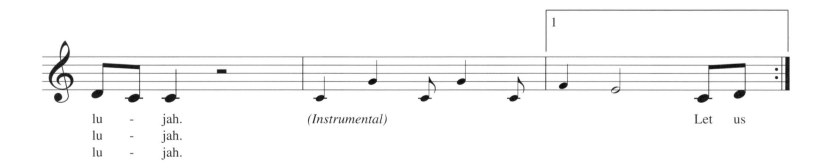

1

lu - jah. *(Instrumental)* Let us
lu - jah.
lu - jah.

2, 3

A - rise, _____

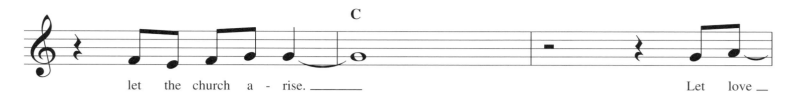

let the church a - rise. _____ Let love _

_ reach to the oth - er side. _____

A - live, _____ come a - live; _

_ let the song _ a - rise. _____

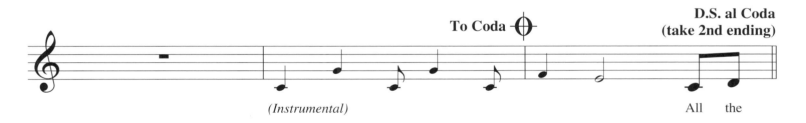

To Coda ⊕   **D.S. al Coda**
(take 2nd ending)

(Instrumental)   All the

CODA ⊕

Ev - 'ry - one sing a new hal - le -

lu - jah. Ev - 'ry - one sing a new hal - le - lu - jah.

NO SWEETER NAME

Words and Music by
KARI JOBE

NOTHING BUT THE BLOOD

Words and Music by
MATT REDMAN

NONE BUT JESUS

Words and Music by
BROOKE FRASER

Worshipfully

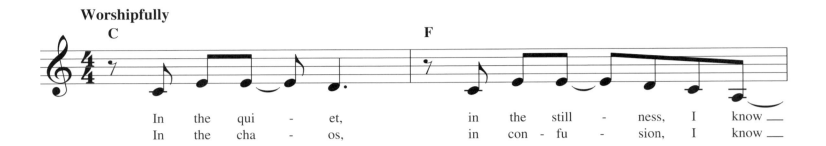

In the qui - et, in the still - ness, I know ___
In the cha - os, in con - fu - sion, I know ___

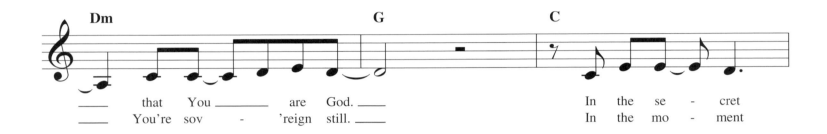

___ that You ___ are God. ___   In the se - cret
___ You're sov - 'reign still. ___   In the mo - ment

of Your pres - ence, I know ___ there I ___ am re - stored. ___   And
of my weak - ness, You give ___ me grace ___ to do ___ Your will.   And

when You call, I won't ___ re - fuse. ___   And
when You call, I won't ___ de - lay. ___

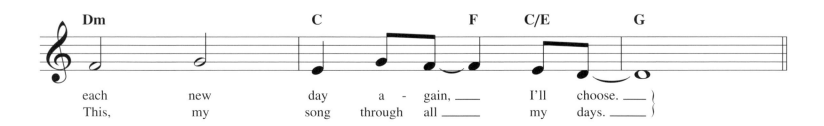

each new day a - gain, ___ I'll choose. ___ }
This, my song through all ___ my days. ___ }

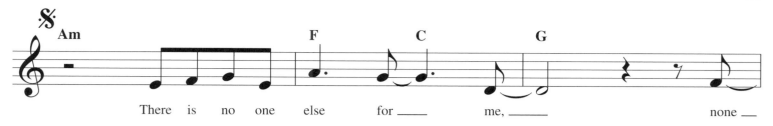

There is no one else for ____ me, ____ none __

____ but Je - sus. Cru - ci - fied to set me ____ free, __

____ now I live ____ to bring Him praise. And all my de - light __

____ is in ____ You, Lord, ____ all of my hope __

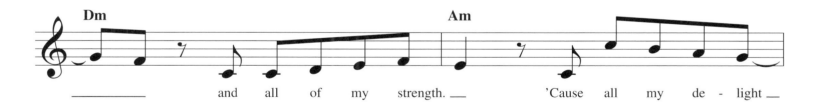

_____ and all of my strength. __ 'Cause all my de - light __

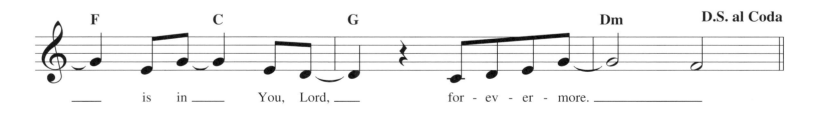

____ is in ____ You, Lord, ____ for - ev - er - more. _____

____ to bring Him praise.

NOT TO US

Words and Music by CHRIS TOMLIN
and JESSE REEVES

117

O PRAISE HIM
(All This for a King)

Words and Music by
DAVID CROWDER

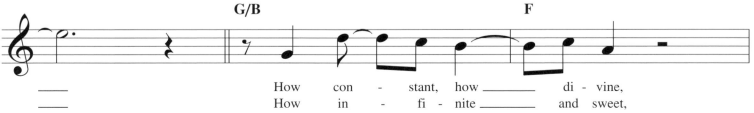

OFFERING

Words and Music by
PAUL BALOCHE

Slowly

The sun can-not com-pare to the glo-ry of Your love. There is no shad-ow in Your

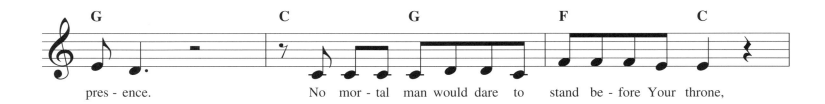

pres-ence. No mor-tal man would dare to stand be-fore Your throne,

be-fore the Ho-ly One of heav-en. It's on-ly by Your blood and it's

on-ly through Your mer-cy, Lord, I come. I bring an

of-fer-ing of wor-ship to my King. No one on earth de-serves the prais-es that I

sing. Je-sus, may You re-ceive the hon-or that You're

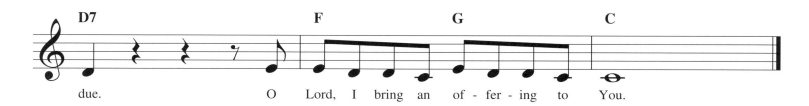

due. O Lord, I bring an of-fer-ing to You.

OUR GOD SAVES

Words and Music by PAUL BALOCHE
and BRENTON BROWN

ONE WAY

Words and Music by JOEL HOUSTON
and JONATHON DOUGLASS

Driving

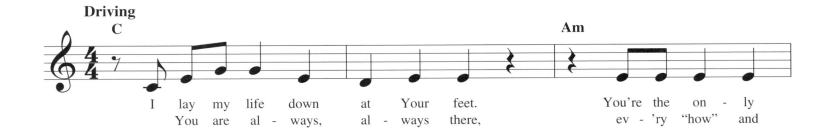

I lay my life down   at   Your   feet.   You're the on - ly
You are al - ways,   al - ways there,   ev - 'ry "how" and

One I need.   I turn to You and You ____ are al - ways   there. ____
ev - 'ry "where."   Your grace a - bounds so deep - ly with - in me. ____

____   In trou - bled times, it's
____   So You will nev - er,

You I seek.   I put You first; that's all I need.
ev - er change;   yes - ter - day, to - day the same,

I hum - ble all I am, ____   all ____ to You. ____
for - ev - er 'til for - ev - er meets ____ no end. ____

123

One way: Je - sus.

You're the on - ly One that I could live for. One way:

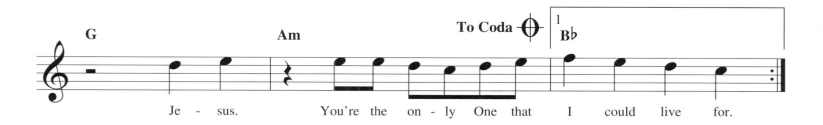

Je - sus. You're the on - ly One that I could live for.

I could live for. You are the Way, the Truth ___ and the Life. We live ___

___ by faith ___ and not ___ by sight ___ for You. ___ We're

liv - ing all ___ for ___ You.

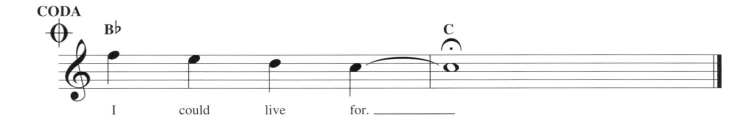

I could live for. ___

OUR GOD

Words and Music by JONAS MYRIN,
CHRIS TOMLIN, MATT REDMAN
and JESSE REEVES

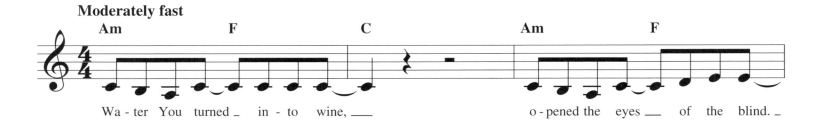

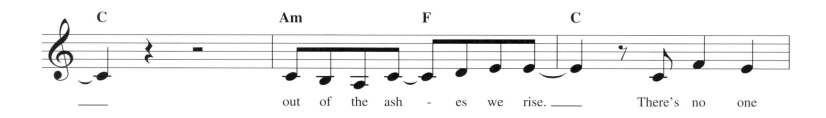

Our God is great - er, our God is strong - er.

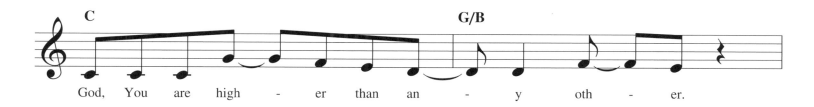

God, You are high - er than an - y oth - er.

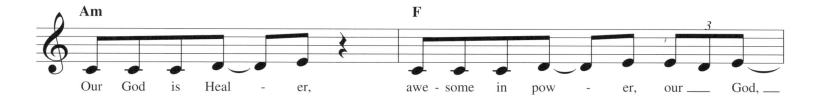

Our God is Heal - er, awe - some in pow - er, our ___ God, ___

___ our ___ God. ___ (Instrumental)

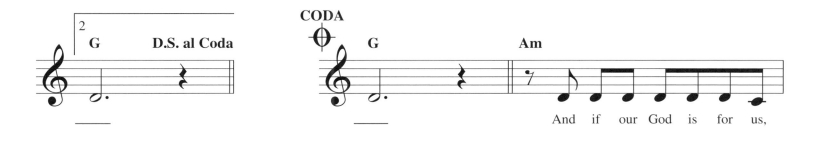

then who could ev - er stop us? And if our God is with us,

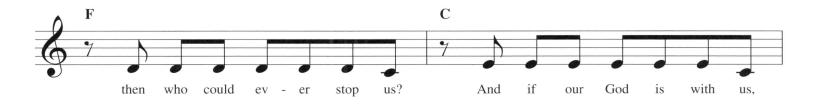

And if our God is for us,

then what could stand a - gainst? ___ And if our God is for us,

then who could ev - er stop us? And if our God is with us, then what could stand a - gainst? _

___ *(Instrumental)* What could stand a - gainst? _

___

Our God is great - er, our God is strong - er. God, You are high - er than an -

- y oth - er. Our God is Heal - er, awe - some in pow - er, our _ God, _

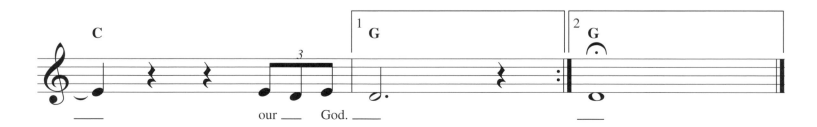

_ our _ God. ___

OVERCOME

Words and Music by
JON EGAN

Slowly, in 2

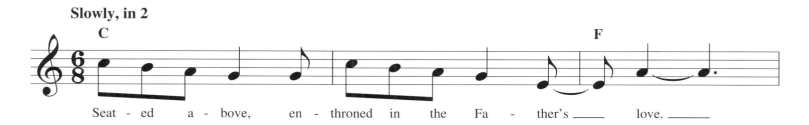

Seat - ed a - bove, en - throned in the Fa - ther's _____ love. _____

Des - tined to die, poured out for all man -

- kind.   God's on - ly Son,
Pow - er in hand,

per - fect and spot - less _____ One.
speak - ing the Fa - ther's _____ plan.

He nev - er sinned, but suf - fered as if He _____ did.)
Send - ing us out, a light in this bro - ken _____ land.)

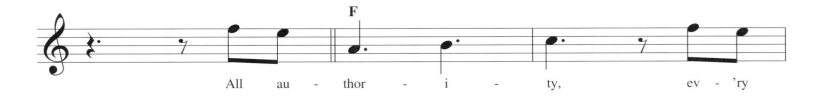

All au - thor - i - ty, ev - 'ry

THE POWER OF THE CROSS
(Oh to See the Dawn)

Words and Music by KEITH GETTY
and STUART TOWNEND

PRAISE ADONAI

Words and Music by
PAUL BALOCHE

RESCUE

Words and Music by
JARED ANDERSON

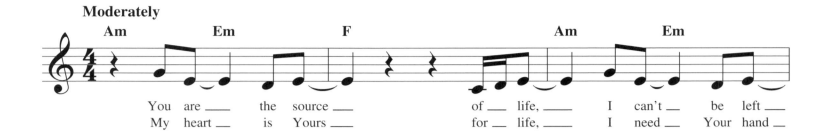

You are ___ the source ___ of ___ life, ___ I can't ___ be left ___
My heart ___ is Yours ___ for ___ life, ___ I need ___ Your hand ___

___ be - hind. ___ No one else will do, ___
___ in ___ mine. ___ No one else will do, ___

I will ___ take hold ___ of You.)
I put ___ my trust ___ in You.)
I need You, Je -

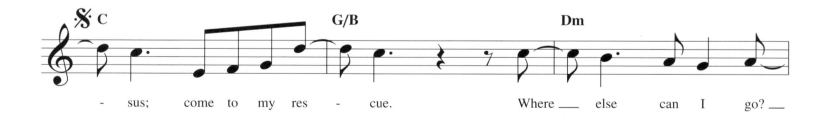

- sus; come to my res - cue.   Where ___ else can I go? ___

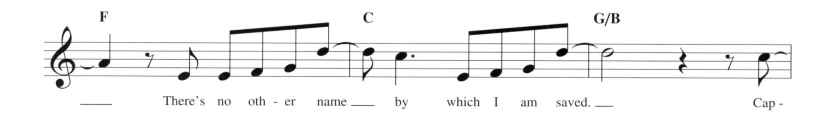

___ There's no oth - er name ___ by which I am saved. ___   Cap -

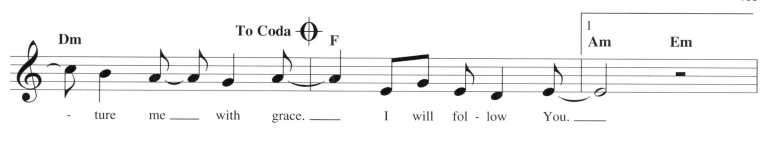

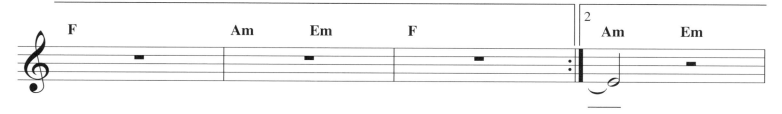

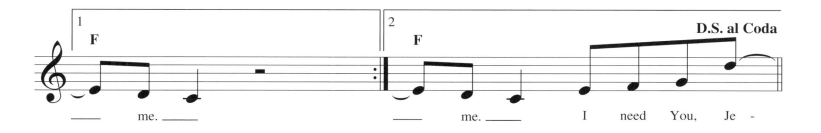

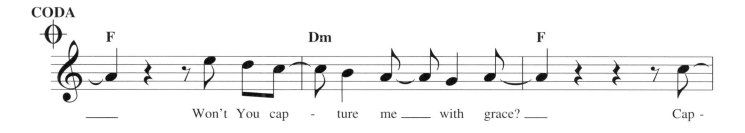

REVELATION SONG

Words and Music by
JENNIE LEE RIDDLE

Slowly

Wor - thy is the Lamb who was slain. Ho - ly, ho - ly is He. ___

Sing a new song to Him who sits on Heav - en's mer - cy seat. ___

Ho - ly, ho - ly, ho - ly is the Lord God Al-might- y, who was and is and is to

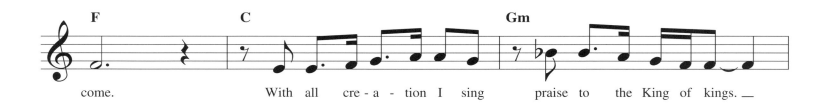

come. With all cre - a - tion I sing praise to the King of kings. __

You are my ev -'ry - thing, and I will a - dore You. _____

To Coda

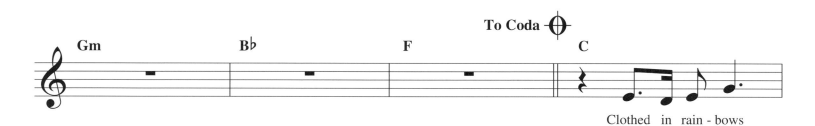

Clothed in rain - bows

SALVATION IS HERE

Words and Music by
JOEL HOUSTON

SPEAK O LORD

Words and Music by STUART TOWNEND
and KEITH GETTY

Moderately slow

Speak, O Lord, as we come to You to re - ceive the food of Your
Teach us, Lord, full o - be - di - ence, ho - ly rev - er - ence, true hu -
Speak, O Lord, and re - new our minds. Help us grasp the heights of Your

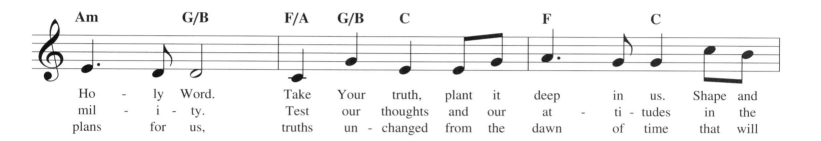

Ho - ly Word. Take Your truth, plant it deep in us. Shape and
mil - i - ty. Test our thoughts and our at - ti - tudes in the
plans for us, truths un - changed from the dawn of time that will

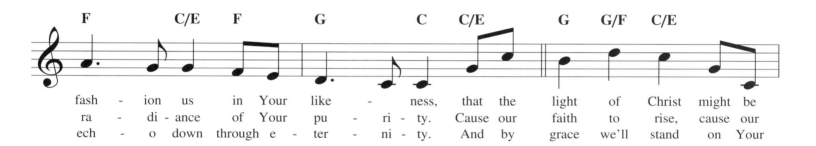

fash - ion us in Your like - ness, that the light of Christ might be
ra - di - ance of Your pu - ri - ty. Cause our faith to rise, cause our
ech - o down through e - ter - ni - ty. And by grace we'll stand on Your

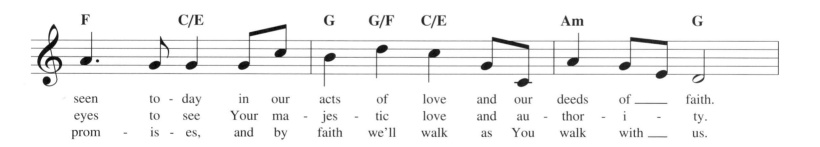

seen to - day in our acts of love and our deeds of _____ faith.
eyes to see Your ma - jes - tic love and au - thor - i - ty.
prom - is - es, and by faith we'll walk as You walk with _____ us.

Speak, O Lord, and ful - fill in us all Your pur - pos - es for Your glo - ry.
Words of pow'r that can nev - er fail; let their truth pre - vail o - ver un - be - lief.
Speak, O Lord, till Your Church is built and the earth is filled with Your glo - ry.

SING, SING, SING

Words and Music by CHRIS TOMLIN,
JESSE REEVES, DANIEL CARSON,
TRAVIS NUNN and MATT GILDER

Sing, sing, sing, ____ and make mu - sic with __ the heav - ens. We __ will

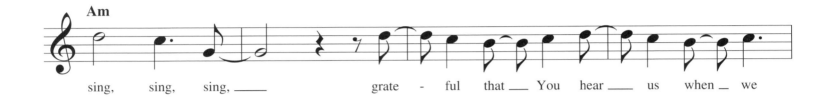

sing, sing, sing, ____ grate - ful that __ You hear __ us when __ we

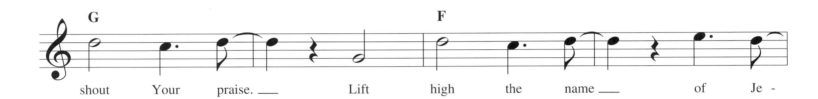

shout Your praise. __ Lift high the name __ of Je -

- sus. __ What's not to love __

__ a - bout __ You? Heav - en and earth ___ a - dore __ You,

kings __ and king - doms bow __ down. Son of God, __ You are __ the One, __

You are __ the One. __

SING TO THE KING

Words and Music by
BILLY JAMES FOOTE

Moderately fast

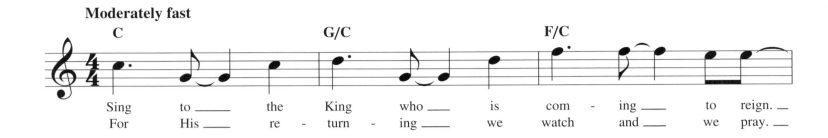

Sing to ___ the King who ___ is com - ing ___ to reign.
For His ___ re - turn - ing ___ we watch and ___ we pray. ___

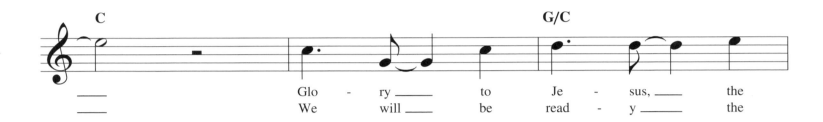

___ Glo - ry ___ to Je - sus, ___ the
___ We will ___ be read - y ___ the

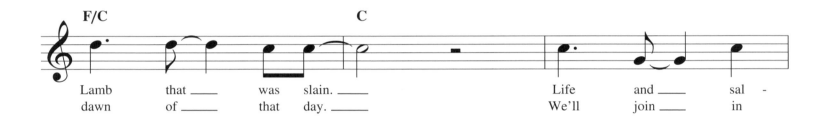

Lamb that ___ was slain. ___ Life and ___ sal -
dawn of ___ that day. ___ We'll join ___ in

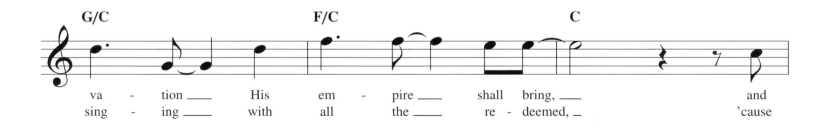

va - tion ___ His em - pire ___ shall bring, ___ and
sing - ing ___ with all the ___ re - deemed, ___ 'cause

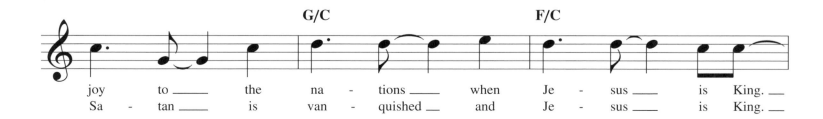

joy to ___ the na - tions ___ when Je - sus ___ is King. ___
Sa - tan ___ is van - quished ___ and Je - sus ___ is King. ___

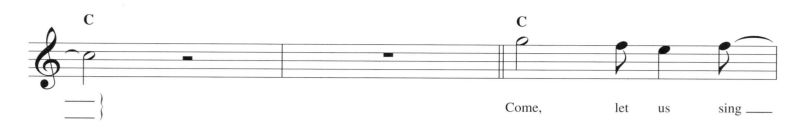

Come,   let   us   sing ___

___ a   song, ___   a   song   de - clar - ing   we ___   be - long ___   to   Je -

- sus,   and   He   is   all   we ___   need. ___

Lift   up   a   heart ___   of   praise. ___   Sing   now   with   voic -

- es   raised ___   to   Je - sus.   Sing   to   the ___

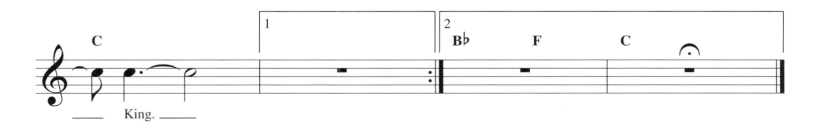

___ King. ___

THE STAND

Words and Music by
JOEL HOUSTON

Moderately slow

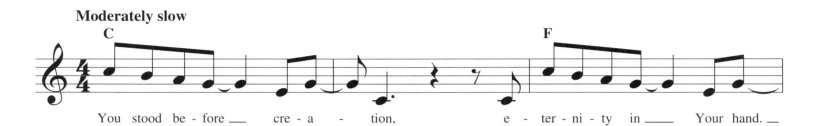

You stood be-fore ___ cre-a-tion, e-ter-ni-ty in ___ Your hand. ___

___ You spoke the earth ___ in-to mo-tion, my soul now ___

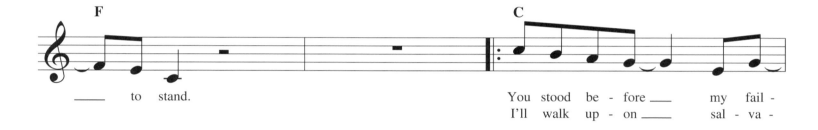

___ to stand.
You stood be-fore ___ my fail-
I'll walk up-on ___ sal-va-

- ure, and car-ried the cross ___ for my shame. ___ My
- tion, Your Spir-it a-live ___ in me, _____ this

sin weighed up-on ___ Your shoul-ders, my soul now ___ to stand.)
life to de-clare ___ Your prom-ise, my soul now ___ to stand.)

So what could I ____ say? ____ And what could I ____ do, __

____ but of - fer this heart, ___ O God, __

com - plete - ly _____ to You. So

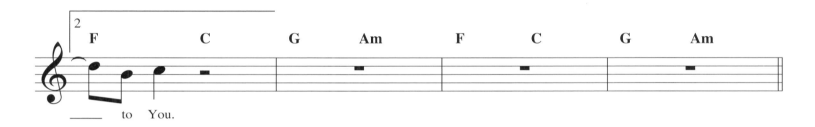

____ to You.

I'll stand with arms high and heart a - ban - doned, in awe of the

One who gave it all. I'll stand, my soul, Lord, to You sur - ren - dered.

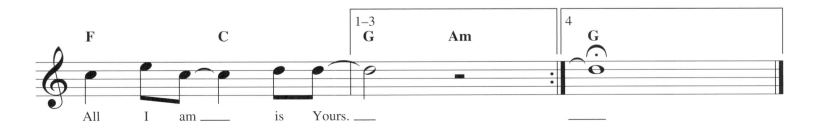

All I am ___ is Yours. ___

STILL

Words and Music by
REUBEN MORGAN

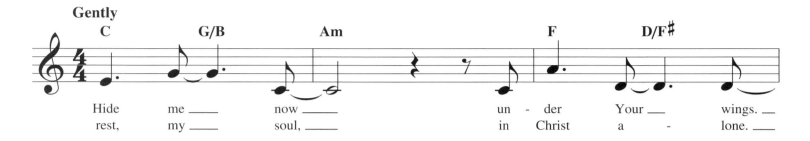

Hide me ____ now ____ un - der Your ____ wings. ____
rest, my ____ soul, ____ in Christ a - lone. ____

Cov - er ____ me ____ with -
Know His ____ pow'r ____ in

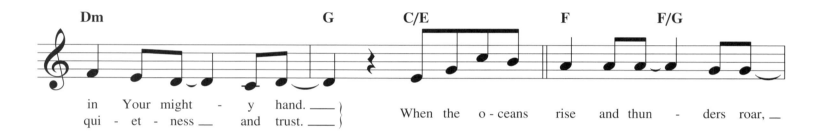

in Your might - y hand. ____ } When the o - ceans rise and thun - ders roar, ____
qui - et - ness ____ and trust. ____ }

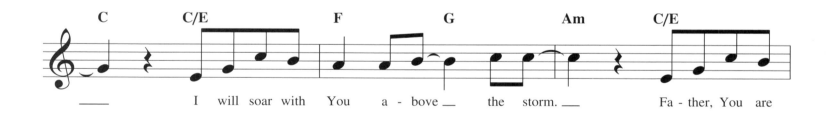

____ I will soar with You a - bove ____ the storm. ____ Fa - ther, You are

King o - ver ____ the flood. ____ I will be still ____ and know You ____ are God. ____

Find

TODAY IS THE DAY

Words and Music by LINCOLN BREWSTER
and PAUL BALOCHE

With excitement

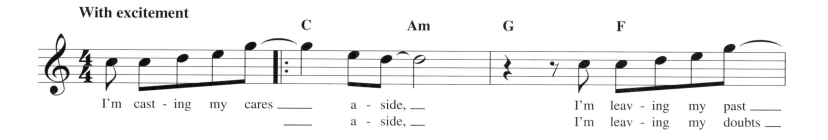

I'm cast-ing my cares ____ a - side, ____ I'm leav-ing my past ____
____ a - side, ____ I'm leav-ing my doubts ____

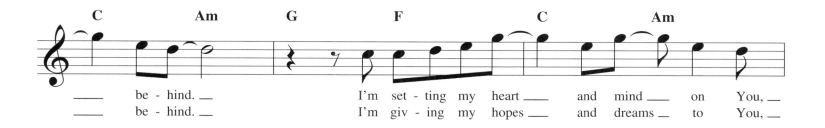

____ be - hind. ____ I'm set-ting my heart ____ and mind ____ on You, ____
____ be - hind. ____ I'm giv-ing my hopes ____ and dreams ____ to You, ____

Je - sus. ____ I'm reach-ing my hands ____
Je - sus. ____

____ to Yours, ____ be - liev-ing there's so ____ much more, ____

know-ing that all ____ You have ____ in store ____ for me ____ is good, ____

_____ is good. _____ To-day is the day _____ You _____ have made; _____

_____ I will re-joice _____ and be glad _____ in _____ it. _____ To-day is the day _____

_____ You _____ have made; _____ I will re-joice _____ and be glad _____ in _____ it. _____

_____ And I _____ won't wor-ry 'bout _____ to-mor-row; I'm

trust-ing in what _____ You say. _____ To-day is the day. _____

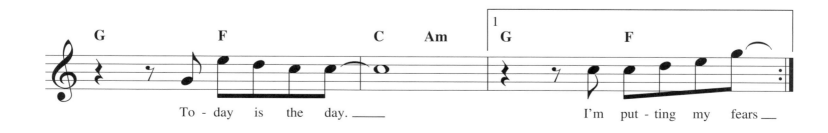

To-day is the day. _____ I'm put-ting my fears _____

147

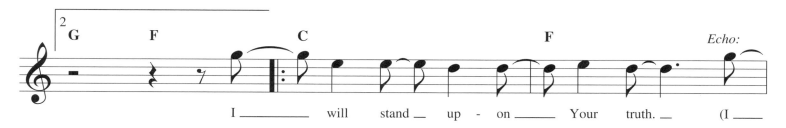

I _____ will stand _ up - on ____ Your truth. _ (I ____

____ will stand _ up - on ____ Your truth.) _ And all ____ my days _ I'll live _

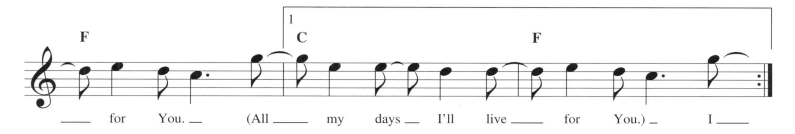

____ for You. _ (All ____ my days _ I'll live ____ for You.) _ I ____

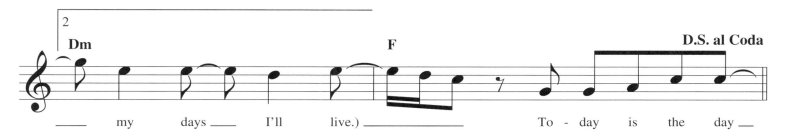

____ my days ____ I'll live.) _____ To - day is the day _

____ to - mor - row; I'm giv - ing You ___ my pain _

____ and sor - row. Where ___ You lead ___ me, I _____ will fol - low. I'm

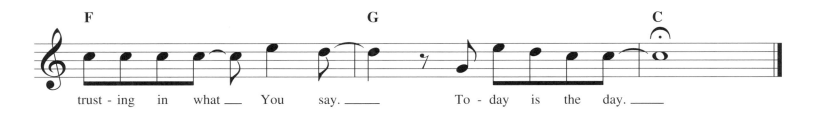

trust - ing in what ___ You say. _____ To - day is the day. ____

STRONGER

Words and Music by BEN FIELDING
and REUBEN MORGAN

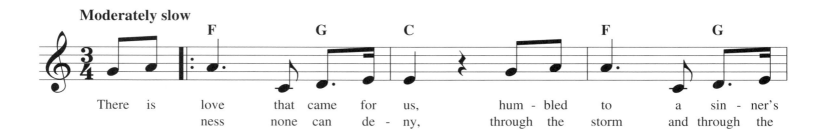

There is love that came for us, humbled to a sinner's
ness none can deny, through the storm and through the

cross. You broke my shame and sinfulness, You rose again victorious
fire. There is truth that sets me free: Jesus Christ, who lives in

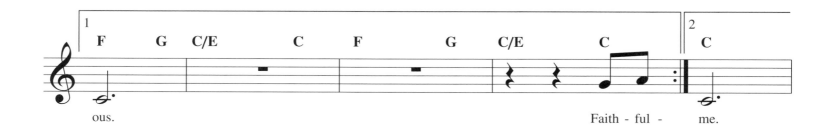

ous.
Faithful me.

You are stronger, You are stronger. Sin is broken, You have

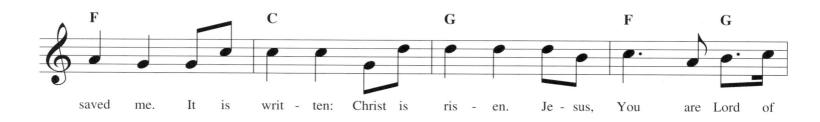

saved me. It is written: Christ is risen. Jesus, You are Lord of

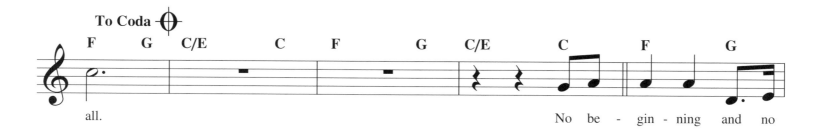

all.
No beginning and no

TAKE IT ALL

Words and Music by MATT CROCKER,
MARTY SAMPSON and SCOTT LIGERTWOOD

Driving

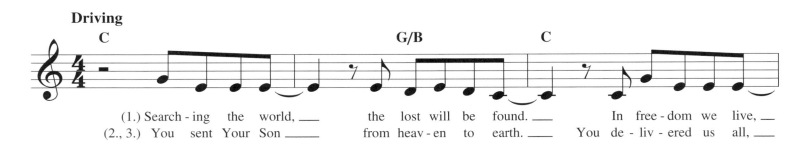

(1.) Search - ing the world, ___ the lost will be found. ___ In free - dom we live, ___
(2., 3.) You sent Your Son ___ from heav - en to earth. ___ You de - liv - ered us all, ___

___ as one we cry out. ___ You car - ried the cross, ___ You died and rose a -
___ it's e - ter - nal - ly heard. ___ I searched for truth, _

gain. My God, I'll on - ly ev - er give my all. ___ and all I found was

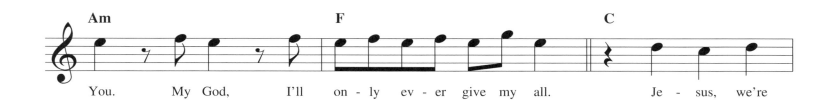

You. My God, I'll on - ly ev - er give my all. Je - sus, we're

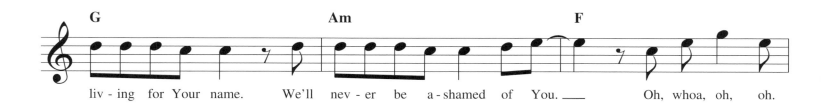

liv - ing for Your name. We'll nev - er be a - shamed of You. ___ Oh, whoa, oh, oh.

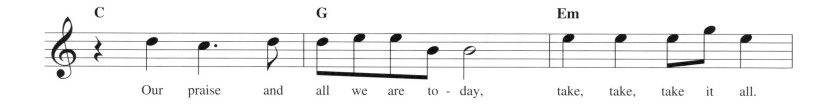

Our praise and all we are to - day, take, take, take it all.

151

TAKE MY LIFE

Words and Music by CHRIS TOMLIN
and LOUIE GIGLIO

Take my life ___ and let _____ it be ___ con - se - crat - ed, Lord,
Take my voice ___ and let _____ me sing ___ al - ways, on - ly, for ___
Take my will ___ and make _____ it Thine, ___ it _____ shall be ___ no long -

___ to Thee. ___ Take my mo - ments and _____ my ___ days, ___ let ___
___ my King. ___ Take my lips ___ and let _____ them __ be ___ filled ___
- er mine. ___ Take my heart, ___ it is _____ Thine _ own, ___ it ___

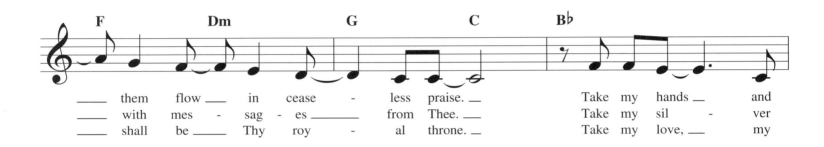

___ them flow ___ in cease - less praise. ___ Take my hands ___ and
___ with mes - sag - es _____ from Thee. ___ Take my sil - ver
___ shall be _____ Thy roy - al throne. ___ Take my love, ___ my

let them move ___ at the im - pulse of _____ Thy love. ___
and my gold, ___ not a mite ___ would I _____ with - hold. ___
Lord, I pour ___ at Your feet ___ its treas - ure store. ___

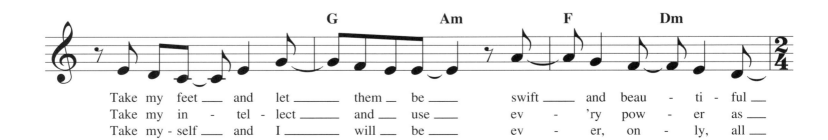

Take my feet ___ and let _____ them __ be ___ swift ___ and beau - ti - ful ___
Take my in - tel - lect _____ and ___ use ___ ev - 'ry pow - er as ___
Take my - self ___ and I _____ will ___ be ___ ev - er, on - ly, all ___

153

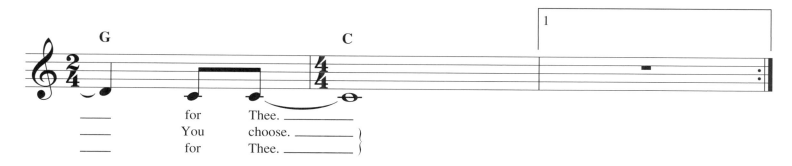

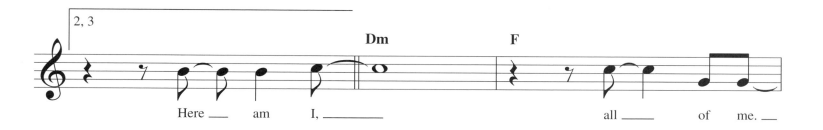

Here __ am I, _____ all __ of me.

__ Take __ my life, _____

it's all __ for Thee. _____

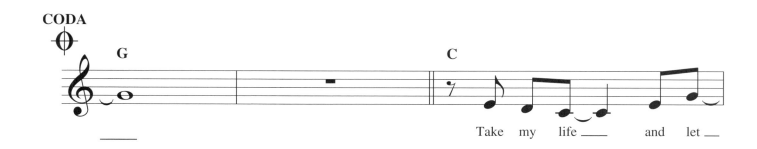

__ Take my life __ and let __

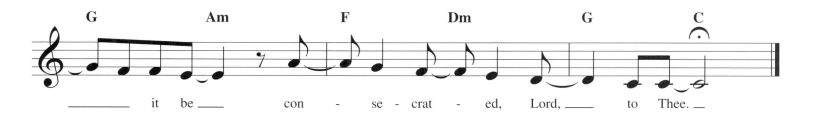

_____ it be __ con - se - crat - ed, Lord, __ to Thee. __

THANK YOU, LORD

Words and Music by PAUL BALOCHE
and DON MOEN

I come be - fore You to - day, ____ and there's just one thing that I ____
For all You've done in my life; ____ You took my dark - ness and gave __

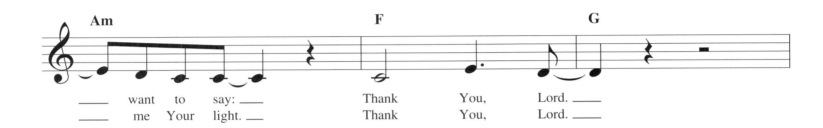

____ want to say: ____ Thank You, Lord. ____
____ me Your light. ____ Thank You, Lord. ____

Thank You, Lord. ____ For all You've giv - en to me, ____
Thank You, Lord. ____ You took my sin and my shame, __

for all the bless - ings that I ____ can - not see, ____
You took my sick - ness and healed ____ all my pain. ____

thank You, Lord. ____ Thank You, Lord. ____
Thank You, Lord. ____ Thank You, Lord. ____

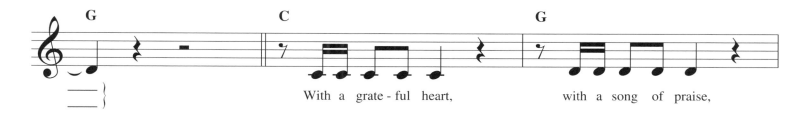

With a grate - ful heart, with a song of praise,

with an out - stretched arm, I will bless Your name. Thank You, Lord. __

__ I just want to thank You, Lord. ____

Thank You, Lord. ____ I just want to thank You, Lord. __

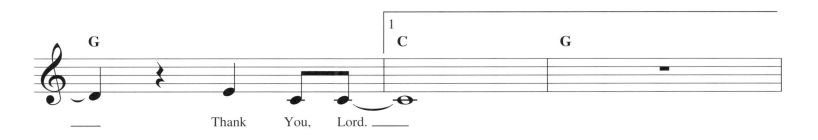

__ Thank You, Lord. ____

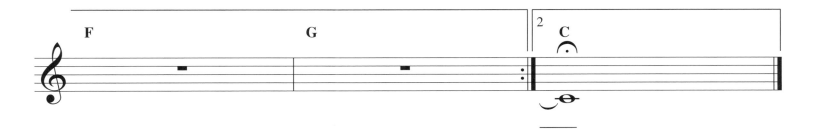

THE TIME HAS COME

Words and Music by
JOEL HOUSTON

Found love be - yond all rea - son. You gave Your life, Your all ___ for ___

___ me,   and called me Yours ___ for - ev - er. ___

Caught in the mer - cy fall - out;   found hope, found life, found all ___ I ___

___ need.   You're all ___ I need. ___   The time ___

___ has come ___ to stand for all ___ we be - lieve ___ in. ___   So I,

___ for one, ___ am gon - na give my praise to You. ___   To - day, ___

UNCHANGING

Words and Music by
CHRIS TOMLIN

Great is ____ Your faith - ful - ness, ____ great is ____ Your faith - ful - ness. ____

____ You nev - er change, __ You nev - er fail, __ O ____ God. __

____ True are ____ Your prom - is - es, ____
____ Wide is ____ Your love and ____ grace, __

____ true are ____ Your prom - is - es. ____
____ wide is ____ Your love and ____ grace. ____

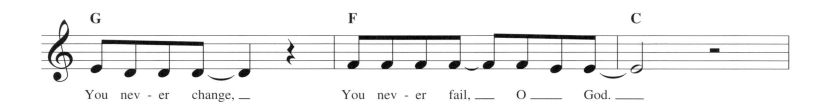

You nev - er change, __ You nev - er fail, __ O ____ God. ____

So, we ____ raise ____ up ho - ly ____ hands ____ to praise ____

WE WANT TO SEE JESUS LIFTED HIGH

Words and Music by
DOUG HORLEY

Driving

We want to see Je - sus lift - ed high, _____ a ban - ner that flies _____ a - cross _____ this land, _____ that all men might see _____ the truth _____ and know _____ He is the way _____ to heav - en. We want to see, we want to see, we want to see Je - sus lift - ed high. _____ We want to see, we want to see, we want to see Je - sus lift - ed high. _____ Step by step we're mov - ing for - ward, lit - tle by lit - tle tak - ing ground. _____ Ev - 'ry prayer _____ a pow'r - ful weap - on, strong - holds come tum - bl - ing down _____ and down _____ and down _____ and down. _____

To Coda

D.C. al Coda (with repeat)

CODA

WONDERFUL, MERCIFUL SAVIOR

Words and Music by DAWN RODGERS
and ERIC WYSE

WONDERFUL MAKER

Words and Music by MATT REDMAN
and CHRIS TOMLIN

Worshipfully

You spread out the skies o - ver emp - ty space, said, "Let there be light;" to a

dark and form - less world Your light was born.

You spread out Your arms o - ver emp - ty hearts, said, "Let there be light;" to a
eye has ful - ly seen how beau - ti - ful the cross, and we have on - ly heard the __

dark and hope - less world Your Son was born.
faint - est whis - pers of how great You are.   You

made the world and saw that it was good.   You sent Your on - ly Son, for You are __

good. What a won-der-ful Mak - er,

what a won-der-ful Sav - ior. How ma-jes-tic Your whis-

- pers, and how hum-ble Your love.

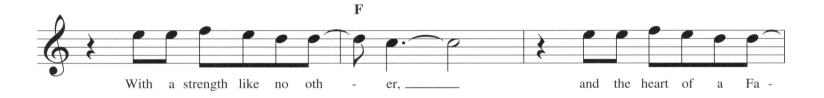

With a strength like no oth - er, and the heart of a Fa-

- ther, how ma-jes-tic Your whis - pers,

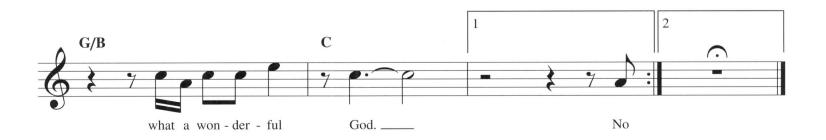

what a won-der-ful God. No

YOU ALONE

Words and Music by JACK PARKER
and DAVID CROWDER

Flowing

1., 3. You _____ are the on - ly _____ One I _____
2., 4. You _____ have giv - en me _____ more than _____

need. _____ I bow all of me _____ at Your _____
I _____ could ev - er have _____ want - ed, _____ and

feet. _____ I wor - ship _____ You a -
I _____ want to give You my _____ heart and my _____

lone. _____
soul. _____

You _____ a - lone _____ are _____ Fa - ther, and You _____

_____ a - lone _____ are _____ good.

You _____ a - lone _____ are _____ Sav - ior, and You _____

YOU ARE GOD ALONE
(not a god)

Words and Music by BILLY J. FOOTE
and CINDY FOOTE

Moderately, in 2

You are not a god cre - at - ed
You're the on - ly God whose pow - er

by hu - man hands. You are not a god de - pend -
none can con - tend. You're the on - ly God whose name ____

- ent on an - y mor - tal man. You are not a
____ and praise will nev - er end. You're the on - ly

god in need ____ of ____ an - y - thing we can give. ____
God who's wor - thy ____ of ev - 'ry - thing we can give. ____

____ By Your plan, that's just the way ____ it is. ____
____ You are God, that's just the way ____ it is. ____

____ You are God ____ a - lone. ____ From be -

YOU ARE GOOD

Words and Music by
ISRAEL HOUGHTON

Brightly

Lord, You __ are good and __ Your mer - cy __ en - dur - eth __ for -

ev - er. __ Lord, You __ are good and __ Your

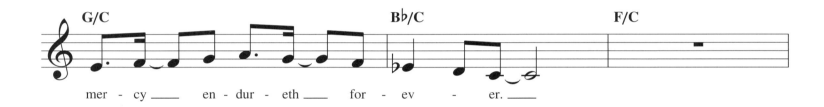

mer - cy __ en - dur - eth __ for - ev - er. __

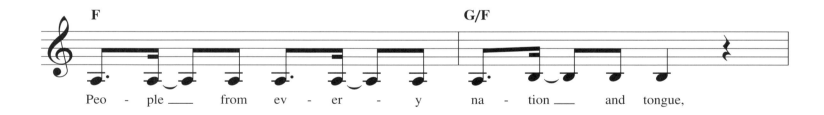

Peo - ple __ from ev - er - y na - tion __ and tongue,

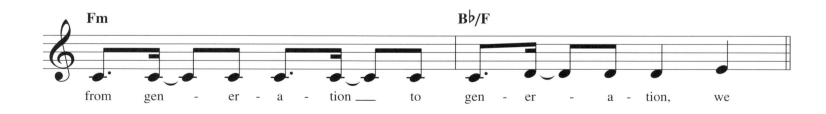

from gen - er - a - tion __ to gen - er - a - tion, we

wor - ship You, __ hal - le - lu - jah, hal - le - lu - jah! We

YOU ARE HOLY
(Prince of Peace)

Words and Music by MARC IMBODEN
and TAMMI RHOTON

With energy

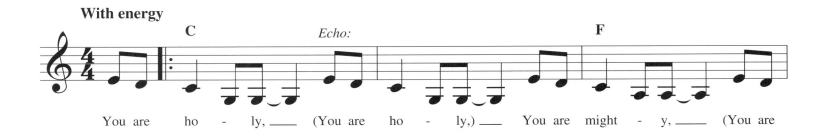

You are ho - ly, ___ (You are ho - ly,) ___ You are might - y, ___ (You are

might - y,) ___ You are wor - thy, ___ wor - thy ___ of
(You are wor - thy,) ___

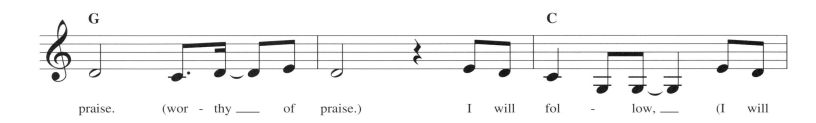

praise. (wor - thy ___ of praise.) I will fol - low, ___ (I will

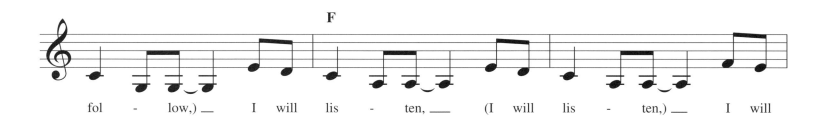

fol - low,) ___ I will lis - ten, ___ (I will lis - ten,) ___ I will

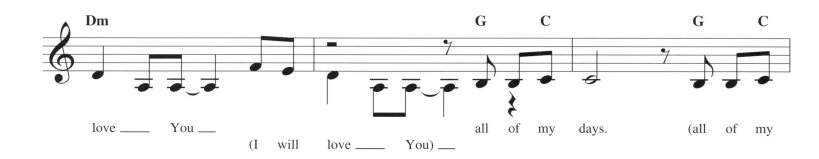

love ___ You ___ all of my days. (all of my
(I will love ___ You) ___

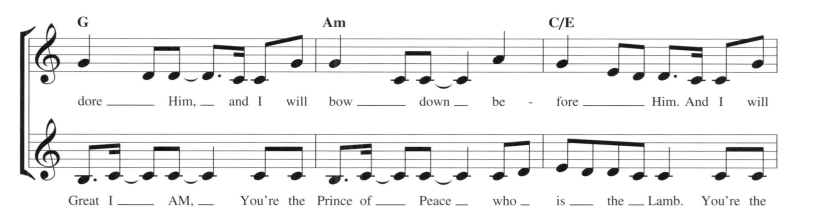

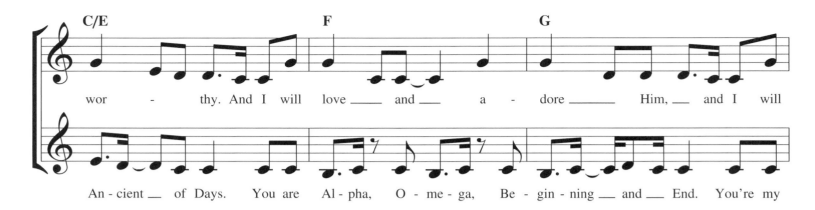

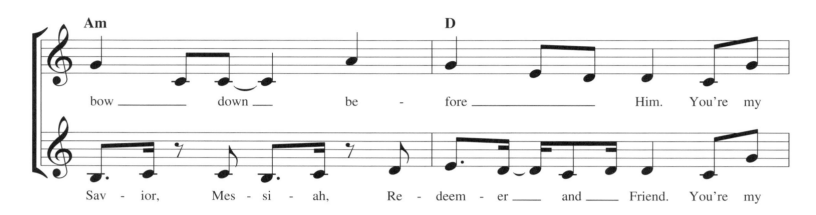

YOUR LOVE OH LORD

Words and Music by MAC POWELL,
MARK LEE, BRAD AVERY,
TAI ANDERSON and DAVID CARR

YOU NEVER LET GO

Words and Music by MATT REDMAN
and BETH REDMAN

Moderately slow

E - ven though I walk through the val - ley of the shad - ow of death, Your
light that is com-ing for the heart that holds on, a

per - fect love is cast - ing out fear. And e - ven when I'm
glo - rious light be - yond all com - pare. And there will be an

caught in the mid - dle of the storms of this life, I
end to these trou - bles, but un - til that day comes, we'll

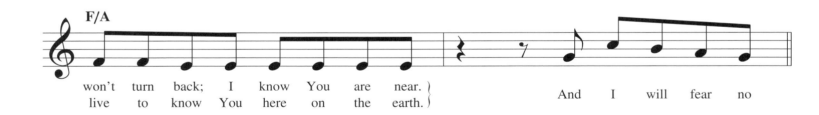

won't turn back; I know You are near.)
live to know You here on the earth.)

And I will fear no

e - vil, for my God is with _____ me.

And if my God is with _____ me, whom then shall I ___

YOU, YOU ARE GOD

Words and Music by
MICHAEL WALKER BEACH

With energy

Here I am; _____ I've come to find _____ You.
Here I am; _____ I've come to thank _____ You.

Here I am _____ to see _____ Your grace, _____
Here I am, _____ a life _____ You've changed. _____

_____ to bring to You _____ an of-
_____ Be - cause You gave _____ Your life _____

- fer - ing. _____ I have to ask _____ my - self _____
_____ for me, _____ You cru - ci - fied _____ Your Son _____

_____ one thing: _____ How can I _____ do an -
_____ for me, _____ how can I _____ do an -

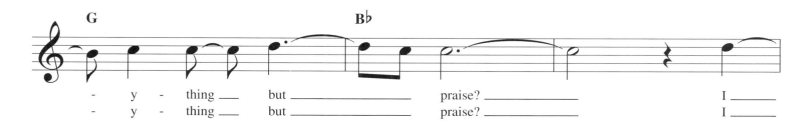

- y - thing ___ but _____ praise? _____ I ___
- y - thing ___ but _____ praise? _____ I ___

___ praise. _____
___ praise. _____ You, You are God, ___

___ You are Lord, ___ You are all ___ I'm liv - ing for. ___

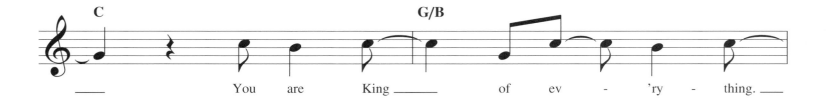

___ You are King ___ of ev - 'ry - thing. ___

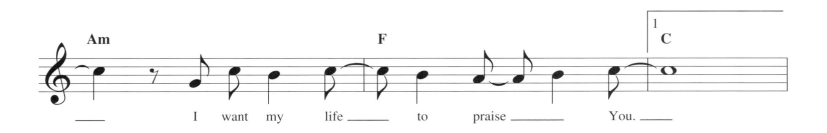

___ I want my life ___ to praise ___ You. ___

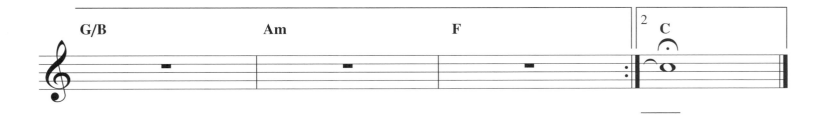

YOU'LL COME

Words and Music by
BROOKE FRASER

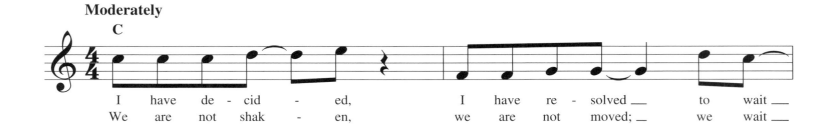

I have de - cid - ed, I have re - solved ___ to wait ___
We are not shak - en, we are not moved; ___ we wait ___

___ up - on ___ You, Lord. ___ My Rock and Re - deem - er,
___ up - on ___ You, Lord. ___ Might - y De - liv - 'rer,

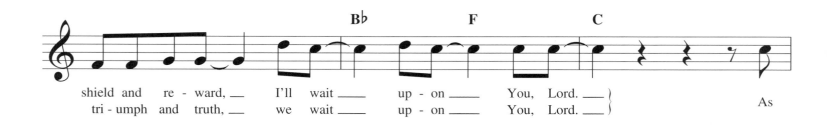

shield and re - ward, ___ I'll wait ___ up - on ___ You, Lord. ___ }   As
tri - umph and truth, ___ we wait ___ up - on ___ You, Lord. ___ }

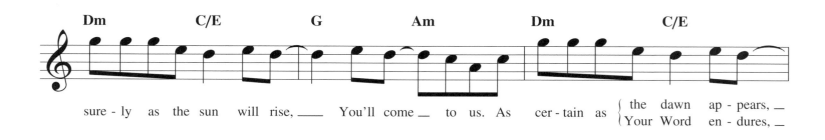

sure - ly as the sun will rise, ___ You'll come ___ to us. As cer - tain as { the dawn ap - pears, ___
{ Your Word en - dures, ___

___ } You'll come. _____ Let Your glo - ry fall as You re -

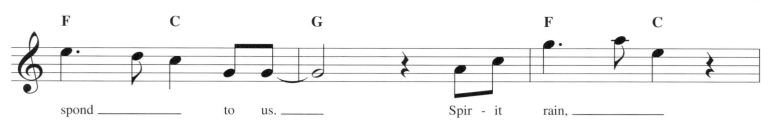

spond _____ to us. _____ Spir - it rain, _____

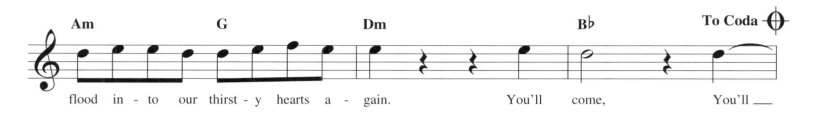

flood in - to our thirst - y hearts a - gain. You'll come, You'll ___

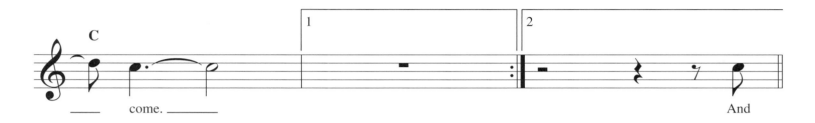

___ come. _____ And

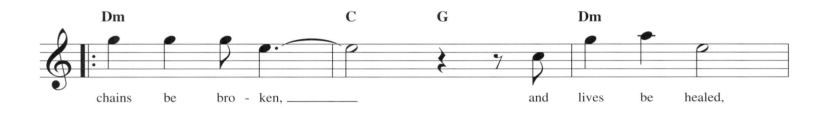

chains be bro - ken, _____ and lives be healed,

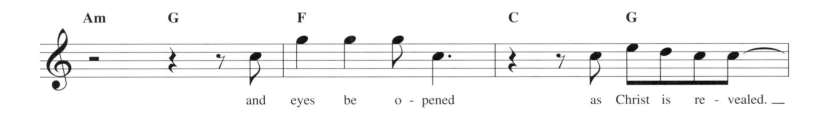

and eyes be o - pened as Christ is re - vealed. __

___ And You'll

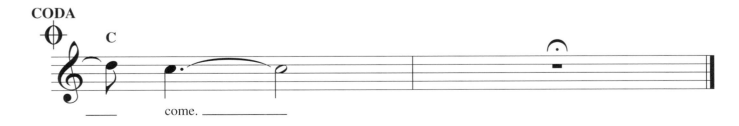

___ come. _____

YOUR GRACE IS ENOUGH

Words and Music by
MATT MAHER

Brightly

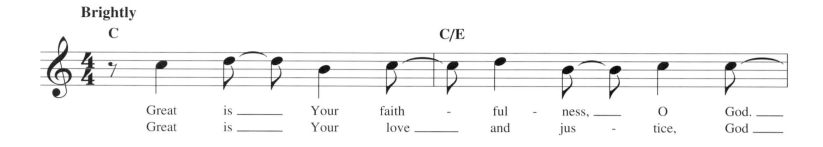

Great is _____ Your faith - ful - ness, _____ O God. _____
Great is _____ Your love _____ and jus - tice, God _____

_____ of Ja - cob.
_____ to lead _____ the strong. _____

You wres - tle with _____
You use _____ the weak _____

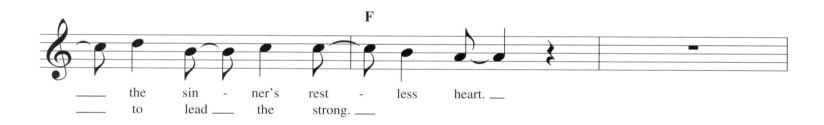

_____ the sin - ner's rest - less heart. _____
_____ to lead _____ the strong. _____

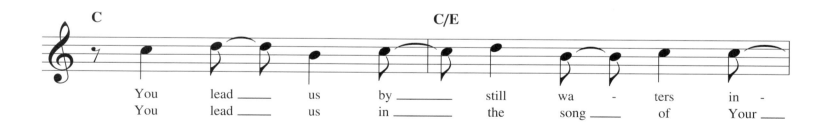

You lead _____ us by _____ still wa - ters in -
You lead _____ us in _____ the song _____ of Your _____

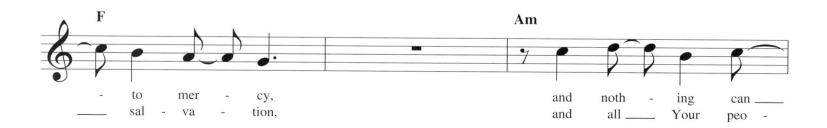

- to mer - cy,
_____ sal - va - tion,

and noth - ing can _____
and all _____ Your peo -

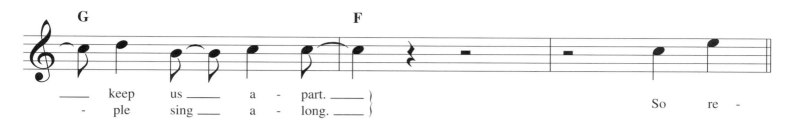

keep us a - part. ____
- ple sing ___ a - long. ___   So re -

mem - ber ____ Your peo - ple, ____ re - mem - ber ____ Your

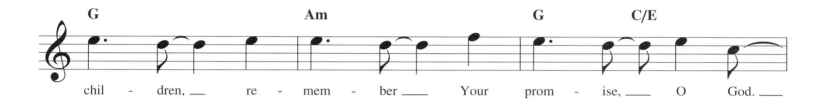

chil - dren, ____ re - mem - ber ____ Your prom - ise, ____ O God. ____

____   Your grace is e - nough, ____

____   Your grace is e - nough, ____   Your

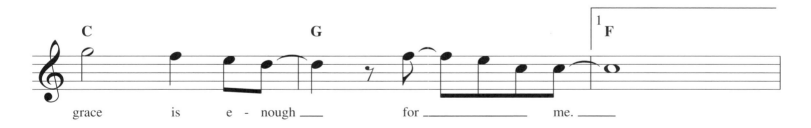

grace is e - nough ____ for _____ me. ____

____   For _____ me. ____

YOUR NAME

Words and Music by PAUL BALOCHE
and GLENN PACKIAM